Seven Stories
that
Sell

Seven Stories *that* Sell

LJ Bloom

Copyright © 2024 by LJ Bloom

All rights reserved. This book, or parts thereof, may not be reproduced in any form without permission.

Paperback ISBN: 979-8-9891641-9-6
Hardback ISBN: 979-8-9891641-7-2
E-book ISBN: 979-8-9891641-8-9

1 3 5 7 9 10 8 6 4 2

To my gorgeous boys—sometimes you wanted a "story from my head," sometimes you wanted to tell me your story. You are, by far, the best story I've ever been a part of—I love you.

CONTENTS

INTRODUCTION	i
PART 1: THE ROLE OF STORYTELLING IN SALES	1
Chapter 1: What Is Storytelling?	3
Chapter 2: What Is Business Storytelling?	11
Chapter 3: The Story of Selling	19
Chapter 4: Selling Through Story	27
Chapter 5: Mistakes, Myths, and Untruths	37
PART 2: THE SEVEN-STORY FRAMEWORK	47
Chapter 6: Introduction to the Seven-Story Framework	49
Chapter 7: The Story of You	59
Chapter 8: The Story of What	69
Chapter 9: The Story of Who	79
Chapter 10: The Experience Story	91
Chapter 11: The Failure Story	103
Chapter 12: The Vision Story	115
Chapter 13: The Proof Story	125
Chapter 14: Wrapping Up	133
ACKNOWLEDGMENTS	139
BIBLIOGRAPHY	141
ABOUT THE AUTHOR	143

Additional resources to support you!

DOWNLOAD THE AUDIOBOOK AND THE SEVEN STORIES TOOLKIT (FOR FREE)!

READ THIS FIRST

Just to say thank you for reading my book, I'd love to share the audiobook version PLUS the accompanying Seven Stories Toolkit, at no cost whatsoever—it's my gift to you.

www.story-coach.com/7-stories-toolkit

Introduction

"We live in story like a fish lives in water. We swim through words and images siphoning story through our minds the way a fish siphons water through its gills. We cannot think without language, we cannot process experience without story."

—Christina Baldwin, author, *StoryCatcher: Making Sense of our Lives Through the Power and Practice of Story*

"ONCE UPON A TIME" is one of the first things we remember in childhood. It's that magical moment when the storyteller—hopefully someone who loves you—gives you all the attention you desire through the telling of a magical world and a hero you imagine you could be.

Maybe it's an elephant who can fly when he holds what he believes to be a magic feather in his trunk. Or perhaps it's a beautiful princess who is banished by her wicked stepmother and left to die in the forest, only to be saved by seven little men. Maybe it's the dreamer who had eleven brothers and was given a beautiful coat of many colors.

We all remember the stories we were told in childhood, but we often miss the lessons they teach us as they seep into our consciousness, and we are left unawares.

For years I have asked people to remember their first storyteller. Usually it's a parent or grandparent, a teacher or a sibling, or maybe it's a rabbi or a priest. Sometimes it's a regular occurrence—a father who would tell a story before bed, a grandmother who would share her stories over the stove as she made the family's favorite dishes, without a recipe, just a bit of this and a pinch of that. Other times it's a rare occasion, an uncle who comes home from a big trip on the other side of the world and tells magical stories of adventures and misdemeanors, always shrouded in excitement and mystery.

There are the people who have no memory of a childhood storyteller, at least initially. Typically, they feel saddened that they can't remember, like they missed out on an important developmental experience (and they may have), but they often later recall their experience of story—a sister who would scare them with stories in bed, or an aunt who would tell something wild, but only after a couple of glasses of wine.

There are the people who eventually realize that they were their own storyteller. Their childhood was filled with solitary moments lost in a novel under the covers reading by flashlight or at the back of the wardrobe in the furthest room from where everyone else would be.

Out of the thousands of people that I've asked about their first storyteller, there are very few who don't fall into any of these categories.

The next question I ask is, "Where did it take place?"

There are a variety of places where storytelling takes place in our childhood memory. First and foremost, it's in the kitchen while preparing or eating food, in the bedroom as we prepare for sleep, and it's as we walk or drive, traveling to a specific destination.

Historically this is the origin of storytelling in every culture. The tribes told stories over the campfire while cooking the food, in the river while cleaning the clothes, at the markets, and to soothe their young. Story is the way we have communicated and connected since the beginning of time.

And the final question that I love to ask is, "How did the story make you feel?"

Sometimes people struggle to articulate how they felt. They share what they did and have trouble finding the emotion behind the action. But inevitably when we dig through our actions and our defenses, we find that we all experienced the very same emotions. Whether I've asked teachers, engineers, coaches or leaders, entrepreneurs, or mothers, we all associate the same emotions with that original experience of story.

We feel excited and interested, maybe even fascinated. We feel curious. We feel seen and heard. We feel special. We feel like we belong.

These are powerful emotions, and they live with us our entire lives in our memory of the moment of being told a story. But it's not just in memory. I discovered that there is a universal and immense power of story in our lives. Through this book, I'll show you how it impacts how we sell in our business too.

PART I

THE ROLE OF STORYTELLING IN SALES

CHAPTER 1
What Is Storytelling?

"Information simply leaves us feeling incompetent and lost. We don't need more information. We need to know what it means. We need a story that explains what it means and makes us feel like we fit in there somewhere."

—Annette Simmons, author of *The Story Factor*

STORYTELLING IS AGE-OLD and exists in every culture, in every country—presumably even before there were countries. In the times of the tribes, people told stories to entertain and to share their experiences. Around the fireside in the evenings, they would share what happened throughout the day; as visitors came to the village, the story of their journey would be told.

Storytelling was not only for entertainment and communication; it was also for education. The elders would tell stories to explain the ways of the tribe to the next generation, the culture to which the children belonged. And the children understood their place in the world by virtue of the stories they were told.

ORIGINS OF STORY

I remember a particular day in school when I was about six years old. The teacher wore a beige wool cardigan that had a scent of flowers and soap. The classroom was warm, and it was story time. I can see myself, settling in for a story, feeling so safe. She opened a book and began to read. I can still feel that sensation in my body, the delight, the adventure, the sheer joy of getting lost in the story.

That feeling of story comes back to me whenever I hear wonderful storytellers, or more commonly when I read a good book. There's nothing I love more than to get lost in the pages of a book where my problems, worries, or anxieties just melt away. Sometimes it's even hard to come back from a good story!

For most of us, the origin of storytelling is at home, in our families and our culture. I often say that being Irish and Jewish, I have a genetic predisposition to being a storyteller! But in truth, story is everywhere, in all cultures and all religions. Some of the best storytellers I've known are priests, rabbis, and other religious and community leaders.

When I asked my client Jacob about his first storyteller, he explained that his father would tell him stories. It wasn't every night, but now and then his father would come to his bedroom, sit on his bed, and tell him a story. It was always about the same character, a little boy who lived in a forest and got up to all kinds of adventures. Jacob loved these stories. Sometimes he would fall asleep before his father finished the story, and he always wanted more. Usually, his father was not very attentive to Jacob; most of the time he seemed to be somewhere else in his mind. But when his father told him the stories about this little boy, Jacob felt like he was there with him in the forest, and it was so exciting. Decades later, Jacob realized that those stories his father used to tell weren't made up. His father was telling him the stories of his own experience as a hidden child in the forests surrounding Berlin during the Second World War.

Years later, I told this story at a conference, on a stage in Las Vegas. When the session was over, an older gentleman came up to me. He had long white hair, a thick white beard, and sparkling eyes. He said to me, "Thank you, thank you, for telling the story about the man whose father was a hidden child in Germany." And then he continued, "It was only when I heard that story that I realized that the stories I've been telling my children and now my grandchildren, the stories that my father told me—they were his real stories, they were the stories of his life—I never realized it until now." He gave me a hug, and said he was so grateful.

You see, we all have origin stories, and it's worth finding out more about yours. This is a starting point for understanding how stories have impacted you, and later you'll be able to see how you can use your stories to impact others.

MODERN STORYTELLING

We have looked at where storytelling comes from, how stories are everywhere, and how they traditionally were all about helping us understand our place in the world. I don't think this has changed at all. We still understand our place in the world by virtue of the stories we're told. There are still the familiar old ways that we tell stories: when we sit together to eat, when we speak on the phone (and now on the computer screen), or if we meet up with people we haven't seen for a while. Occasionally we even send letters!

I grew up in Ireland in a traditional Jewish family, where stories were often told over meals. Friday night particularly was when the family got together—my siblings, my parents, my grandmothers, and any stray family, friends, or my father's work colleagues who were free and had no plans. The conversation was lively and provocative. Though no one ever said it out loud, we were always trying to shock my grandmothers. When I think back, I'd say we were a particularly opinionated bunch; everyone had something to say.

As the youngest in the family, I would have to try hard to get my voice heard. No wonder I became a storyteller and speaker—finally someone would listen to me! Much later, I realized that the secret to great storytelling is in the listening, not the telling (I had a lot to learn).

We would share stories of the things we had experienced during the week. Someone would inevitably disagree with someone else's viewpoint and we would dive into a discussion. Sometimes a book would be pulled out from the bookshelf to prove a point, and often there would be some teasing and someone's idea or opinion would be bashed.

To this day I miss this kind of banter, these kinds of stories. Until I left Ireland, I don't think I realized the ease with which Irish people can share stories, at least on the surface. The gift of the gab is a real thing; even now I can meet a random Irish person on the street, and we find what to speak about for a lengthy round of storytelling, even if we say very little and have no prior knowledge of each other. Then we might walk away and never speak again.

As a teenager, I would spend hours on the phone. In the evening I'd call the very friends I had spent the entire day with, and we'd share more stories (not that I can remember for the life of me what we'd say). Of course, the phone had a cord, so I'd sit on the floor with my back to the radiator, unable to move around or do anything else. With my back warm and the phone glued to my ear, I'd spend hours there, until someone would yell that they needed the phone, or my dad would complain about the phone bill "and for goodness sake, give it a break!"

It's funny, nowadays I can't imagine just speaking on the phone without doing anything else at the same time. My phone calls happen when I'm walking my dog, hanging laundry, or cooking—a conversation during chores or while driving to a destination. It seems we have lost the ability just to speak to each other, without other distractions or activities.

It was the way we did business too. In my first few jobs, we'd have to factor in time to get to know our colleagues and our clients. And that happened by telling stories over meals or drinks, usually after hours and sometimes with a thin line between what was work and what was appropriate. Early in my career I took a vow never to drink with business colleagues! Such was the story of business in those days.

Though these ways all still exist, there are new ways to tell stories too.

Recently, I told a bunch of stories for an interview I was asked to do. The host had worked with me over a decade ago and was now looking for new material for her podcast, so she reached out. We spent about an hour together, sharing stories about our lives, our work, and the topic she wanted to explore. Interestingly, the most important moment of the interview was when I recalled a story she had told me a decade before. We hadn't spoken in the time in between and yet I still remembered her story. That is the power of story.

We tell stories through social media too, of course. I know many people say that you *must* use social media, and there is a time and place for it, but I have to say it's not something that comes naturally to a lot of us. Though it can be very addictive, I've often had the experience where I've started to follow a story on social media, only to be disgusted by how manipulated I've felt ten minutes later when the story ends. This is not the kind of story I'll be sharing here, so don't worry!

The truth is that the medium or modality that you use for storytelling is not important. There are many to choose from and, depending on your audience, they can boost your business or destroy it. What's important is the kind of story you tell and how appropriate and relevant it is for your audience.

So, ultimately, modern storytelling is not different from the stories of old, assuming you are telling authentic, relevant, and true stories. It's a tall order, but I've got you and we're going to figure out how to do just that!

TRUTH AND FICTION ABOUT STORY

Stories have been selling us stuff forever. There's no argument about that. Since the beginning of time, or at least the beginning of consumption and advertising, we have been sold everything you can imagine with a story.

When my father was a young man, he decided to leave Ireland to find his fortune in Canada. He was something of an entrepreneur, having left school very early to help his father in his business. After a few years, he set sail to the promised land of Montreal, Quebec. He loved it there and quickly got his dream job with Jaguar—he had always loved cars and had spent most of his weekends racing them around the Dublin mountains.

He was quite happy in Canada. His life was good. I believe he was getting ready to build a life there. Then one day, so the story goes, his mother called him up and told him that his father was very sick, and he needed to come home. Always the dutiful son, my father quit his job and made immediate arrangements to return to Ireland. When he arrived, he found his father no sicker than he had been before he left. And his mother? Well, she told him, "All's fair in love and war. I wanted you home." So home he was. A few weeks later he met my mother, and the rest, as they say, is history.

This was a story I grew up with, and for years I never thought about what it meant. I knew my grandmother had a fierce love for her youngest son and would do anything for him, and for us too, though she always did it her way and got her own way! I grew up with my grandmother's stories, and as she became senile she told stories from her teenage years in great detail and remembered every word of the songs she sang along to on the radio, but she had trouble remembering who we were or what she had done five minutes before.

As a result of this story, I knew that my father would never interfere with the plans I might have to travel and see the world, or where I might decide to settle. I knew that Canada—and Montreal in particular—is a wonderful, exciting, and beautiful place. And I knew that stories were powerful enough to manipulate the people you most love and get your way no matter what!

I always say that stories are age-old; they've been around forever, "since the beginning of time." Well, it's also true that stories for selling have been around for a long time. My earliest memories are of advertising "stories," making us believe that we would not survive childhood without drinking milk every day, that Coca-Cola was the key to youth and happiness, and that smoking was cool and then it was very much not. We have been manipulated by stories so that people, corporations, and governments could get rich without much thought or motivation about the health and wellness of those consuming the goods that have been "storied" into us over the generation.

But these are not the stories I want to focus on. The manipulation, the bad intent—it's not the story world that I live in, nor is it the one I want to share with you. Together we will explore stories for good, stories that create meaning and enrichment, stories that impact and change the world. Are you ready?

CHAPTER 2
What Is Business Storytelling?

> *"Although businesspeople are often suspicious of stories . . . the fact is that statistics are used to tell lies and damned lies, while accounting reports are often BS in a ball gown. . . . If a businessperson understands that his or her own mind naturally wants to frame experience in a story, the key to moving the audience is not to resist this impulse but to embrace it."*
>
> —ROBERT MCKEE, author of *Story: Substance, Structure, Style and The Principles of Screenwriting*

THE CEO APPROACHED THE PODIUM, cleared his throat, and started fiddling with the overhead projector. (I've dated myself here of course—this was the old days of business—but why he couldn't have had someone check the projector before he went up, or do a dry run before the 170 employees were sitting in the audience waiting for him to start, I have no idea.) Anyway, he cleared his throat again and began to speak about what a phenomenal year the company had had, with outstanding results. He started reasonably well but then began to churn through the numbers, without any context or connection to his audience.

I looked around the room. At first people were really interested; there was a genuine buzz that wasn't just about taking a few hours off, getting the posh sandwiches, and the impatiently awaited gift (one year it had been a fancy organizer). Here's the thing, though: within minutes of him starting to speak, you could feel the energy wane and the interest die out. By the third slide, people were clearly slumped and there was that hopeless feeling of "when can we get out of here" in the air.

Quite a few years later, I attended a similar event. It began with that feeling of anticipation and excitement, but this time the CEO had the tech sorted out and, more importantly, he had a fantastic story. He talked about individuals in the room and how they had outperformed expectations, asking everyone to cheer. He talked about the story of the product and some of the clients. He shared about the moment they thought that all was lost when a production flaw emerged, but how one of the teams had saved the day. It was riveting, and there was thunderous applause as he finished his talk.

What a difference!

Whatever you're doing in business, if you have a story that is relevant to your audience—whether it's your employees, your clients, your investors, or even your spouse—the story will do the work. By "do the work," I mean the story will help you get the result you desire: the commitment, the sale, the funding, and the support. Whatever it is you need from the person listening, the story is the way to make it clear, compelling, and powerful.

When you can discover, craft, and tell compelling stories, it becomes a superpower. The great news is that you don't need any special talent to be able to do this. *Everyone* can tell a story!

WHY TELL STORIES?

It was winter and I was basically single parenting my three very young children as my partner was working overseas. He would come home every second weekend, and inevitably when he was away, the

Chapter 2: What Is Business Storytelling?

kids would be sick. We had just moved to a new country, so we were all getting used to the new bugs and viruses.

My friend had invited me to a storytelling evening, though an evening out seemed impossible. I did manage to find a sitter and made it to the hall just as a woman walked up to the stage and a man grabbed his guitar and joined her. They started to tell stories. I couldn't believe it; it was almost shocking. I had this visceral feeling, a sense of excitement and recognition. *Oh, this is who I am; this is what I need to do.* I was drawn to storytelling, realizing that this is what I had been doing all these years but had never really noticed.

I had been telling stories in my workshops and training sessions in my corporate job for the previous decade. But I never called it storytelling; it was just that thing I did—the thing that made people pay attention and engage, the thing that helped them learn and grow. Storytelling was in my blood, and I had never noticed.

In the break at that evening event, I went up to the woman and said, "I heard you have a course, and I'd like to join it."

"Great," she said. "That would be lovely."

"No, I mean now, I want to start now. Please let me pay you!" It felt so urgent that I didn't want to waste any more time. I needed to learn everything I could about this thing called storytelling.

Have you ever known so clearly, so truly, that something was right for you? I'm guessing you have; most of us have who have started a business.

I began learning how to tell stories and to become a storyteller, and it was around then that I was doing a course in coaching. I wanted to explore coaching in a more formal way and that meant I'd decided to learn and get a certification. (I'm a sucker for doing things "the right way.") As I studied both storytelling and coaching simultaneously, I started to notice the similarities. The experience of great storytelling was not so different from the experience of great coaching, and there were similar skills required for both.

The day I started googling "story coach," my hands were shaking. It seemed like such a revelation to me, and yet there was almost nothing online that was related. I started buying domain names. I knew I was onto something.

That's when I started my business Story Coach, and very soon I realized that even if I was a fantastic storyteller and a brilliant coach, I needed to get clients if I was to make a success of it. Though I had realized the connection between coaching and storytelling for the purpose of coaching, I was only at the start of my journey to understand the importance of storytelling for business growth.

What I came to understand is that when stories are involved, people listen, connect, and remember what you say. And that matters in business because it helps you articulate what you do in a way that's compelling and attractive so that clients start to hear about you and resonate with your story. It also helps you differentiate what you do from others who offer a similar service. You might be thinking that differentiation is not all that important to you. However, if you think you're in a field that has little competition, then it's one of two things. Either you're a very early adopter and it's only a matter of time before other practitioners get wind of your brilliant idea and start to use it and become competition, or your idea, though it may seem great, is not viable as a business and therefore others have either tried and failed or not tried at all. So we must assume that either now or soon, you will have a lot of competition with what you do. That means you need to differentiate your service and your offer from all the others that look and sound similar.

A brilliant way to do so is by telling your story. No one has the same story as you. No person has the exact same set of experiences, education, worldview, and expertise as you do. This means that only you can tell your story and your story is different from everyone else's. And that's great news, but it's only the start; you need to find out how your approach and your perspective is different so you can show up with something really interesting to offer. Your point of view is a wonderful differentiator, and it should be embedded. And of course, you need to articulate all of this through a powerful story.

WHO CARES?

You may be wondering who wants to hear your story. Lots of people have told me that. Or perhaps you're thinking that if you haven't had a near-death experience, then what story could you possibly tell that would be interesting enough? Well, most of us have not had near-death experiences, thank goodness, yet we all have great stories. If you have lived, you have a story to tell.

I remember visiting a corporate client. The minute I arrived she started telling me about an inspirational speaker that had come to the company the day before. She said to me, "You'd have loved it; he had such an amazing story." And she proceeded to tell me about this incredible fighter pilot who had to eject from his plane, ended up in a coma for months, was expected to die but managed to regain consciousness, and began to heal. Ultimately, he became an outstanding athlete and competed in the Special Olympics.

Now, I'd heard of this speaker before and he really does have an exceptional story. What an amazing person, with incredible resilience and talent. I truly admire him. His story is astounding and I've been told that he shares amazing insights into day-to-day living, his deep appreciation for the gifts we all have, and powerful lessons on resilience. However, though I admire the person and acknowledge his fascinating story, I believe his story will always stay in the realm of the unattainable. It's hard to relate to a story like this because I don't feel like it meets my life in any way. Yes, I can learn from his insights, just like I might learn from a Tibetan monk who's spent the last forty years in meditation and prayer, but I'm not going to go retire into the nearest cave.

These inspirational stories have an important role to play, but we should also celebrate the stories that we can all actually reach and relate to. These are the stories of everyday life that show how "normal" people can experience unexpected learning and insight even though nothing particularly dramatic happened. It's just normal life, but everyone can relate to it.

These are the stories that turn the mundane into magic. These are the stories we can all experience, craft, and tell. They are the stories that not only inspire us but also impact and change us. I believe that all stories should be told, but not necessarily in your business. Some stories should be told to your family, your partner, your colleague, or your therapist. And then there are stories that should be told in your business.

So do people really care about your story? Yes, but only if the story is relevant. In fact, we all have intense curiosity about the stories of others. It's why we spend so much time on social media, why we "follow" others, and love to be "followed," so that we can watch the story play out and share our story with others.

It's really about connection. We crave connection with ourselves and others and storytelling is how we reach out and how we connect.

That's the crux of it—stories connect us to others and help us make meaning. In fact, story is the ultimate meaning maker and, in a time where we strive to understand our reality, taking control of our own story is so important.

PERSUASION AND INFLUENCE

Donal was a good friend. I loved that he was enthusiastic and super positive, a real go-getter. So when he came to me raving about a scheme, of course I was going to give him the benefit of the doubt. He was so excited by how much money he had made and how it was changing the lives of so many people. He told me story after story of the people he now knew who were involved and the difference it had made to them. I remember he spoke about Shirley, who had been struggling as a single mother, working three different jobs and still not always making her rent. She had joined the group and was now a team leader and making a ton of money. I was persuaded.

To cut a long and painful story short, it was a kind of pyramid scheme, and I lost every penny. Donal is still a friend, and we don't talk about it; I imagine he has regrets. But in truth it was the story that got me! When he told me all about himself and others, the lives that had been transformed, I knew that he believed it, that it was true for him. And I believed it too.

Stories possess a remarkable power to sway hearts and minds. They can be used for good and for bad, intentionally or accidentally. It's a huge responsibility, let's understand why.

Stories resonate with our emotions. When we hear a compelling story, it moves us beyond our rational thinking to touch our hearts. Whether the story is joyful or sad, full of hope or fear, we feel the emotion and connect with the storyteller and the protagonist of the story. It's very persuasive!

The relatability of the story is what makes such a difference. When the characters in the story are recognizable, they remind us of our own experiences and struggles. We see ourselves in their shoes and so the message becomes so much more tangible and urgent.

Compelling stories command our attention and as we follow the characters and the plot, they become imbedded in our memory. We may even be less discerning about the facts as we are caught up in the story.

Similarly, a well-told story builds trust. When the story feels authentic (and we can't fake authenticity), we believe the story and so are persuaded by the experience. We are engaged in the images of the story as we visualize what's happening and those vivid mental images make the story more real to us.

CHAPTER 3

The Story of Selling

"If we are going to be part of the solution, we have to engage the problems."
—Majora Carter, urban revitalization strategist
and public radio host

I WALKED INTO THE STORE with the vague idea of buying a sweater. I'm not a very good shopper; I'm far too self-conscious and don't usually like what I see in the mirror. Most often I'm attracted by the colors and, though I've spent years wearing black, I love color. I'm always drawn to the reds, oranges, and blues. On this particular day, there was a stunning red dress hanging up at the entrance of the store and I immediately walked towards it. The saleswoman followed my eyes and started to tell me how gorgeous the dress was and how it would suit me perfectly. I agreed to try it on and already noticed in the dressing room that it felt uncomfortable. The saleswoman drew me out to look in the mirror and was all over me about how beautiful it looked. Now, as I said, I don't like shopping and I always dress for comfort. I want style too, but not at the expense of comfort.

Well, this dress was gorgeous, but it didn't fit me well. It was tight around my upper arms and too loose around the neck. The saleswoman was not deterred. She was convinced that nothing would look better on me. It was incredibly stressful. What was clear to me was that she was going for the sale, not for customer satisfaction, and certainly not for truth. The dress did not look good on me at all!

Of course, I did not buy the dress, but you know what? I didn't go back into that store again either. I hate that kind of selling.

This story, and others like it, are the reason that businesspeople get really hung up about selling. It's one of the biggest barriers to success in business and it's time to dive deep to understand it, figure it out, and find a solution.

WHY WE HATE SELLING

There are several reasons we hate selling, so let's break it down.

- **Prior experience:** As I discussed above, we've all had experiences of being sold something we didn't want or need. It's uncomfortable at best, and breeds distrust in the individual, the brand, and even entire industries at worst. For years I've had a love-hate relationship with online entrepreneurs because I've experienced many of them using attractive language and slick technology to trick people into buying substandard programs. While I was interested in the promises they made, they were often far from what was delivered. This and stories like it have bred distrust in the entire online personal development industry, and the same can be said for online financial services, where there are more scams and tricks than credible options. It can be a scary, uncharted world online, and you need to be justifiably cautious as you navigate it.

- **Negative stereotypes:** We've all heard of the sleazy car salesman who will sell his grandmother (or his soul) faster than a real deal in an automobile! There are all kinds of sales stereotypes that depict the very act of selling as being slimy or sleazy and no one wants to be perceived that way. The irony is that most of us love to buy; it's quite a rush. In fact, people talk about "retail therapy," because that's how good it feels to spend money and buy something you love. Despite that, we still find that we are distrustful of salespeople and assume that they will be sleazy. As an extension to this thinking, we start to believe that if we dare to sell something, then we'll inevitably behave in the same unethical way. This makes no sense. Why would our entire personality and value system suddenly just disappear because we want to sell something? The icing on this inedible cake is that we often don't even notice when we have a good sales experience that we can learn from and emulate.

- **Fear of rejection:** Intense anxiety about rejection and ostracism drives many people's fear of selling. The thought of a customer rejecting them as an individual, rather than just rejecting their offer, can be daunting. Many entrepreneurs consider their work as a part of themselves. They tend to overidentify with their work and conflate it with their own sense of innate value. As part of their development as a new business owner, they need to disconnect themselves from their offer so that when a potential client decides not to buy, it doesn't feel like a personal rejection. For many entrepreneurs who consider themselves heart centered and value driven, a rejection of their program or service can feel like a rejection of the very thing they value most about themselves, their choices, and even their lifestyle. This causes significant resistance to them even learning how to sell.

- **Pressure:** When you need the sale, it's hard not to feel desperate and to communicate this energy to your potential sale. And as a start-up entrepreneur, you pretty much always need the sale. The attachment to the outcome, to the revenue coming in, causes a huge amount of stress, tension, and failure in business. The stakes just feel too high. If you don't make the sale, and then the next one, it's possible that you might not be able to pay rent that month. That's a lot of pressure. And it takes a toll on your ability to show up to the potential client enthusiastically and openly.

  Some of the easiest sales I've ever made were when I genuinely didn't need, or particularly desire, to make the sale. But it's hard to be in this position when you're starting out, or when you're not as flush financially as you'd like to be. The problem is that each sale becomes much more than it really is. It's like we exaggerate the meaning of each interaction, imposing catastrophic implications. This is not a good recipe for actually making sales.

- **Misconception:** Some people really believe that selling is manipulation. At times it can be, but often it's not. If we associate selling with convincing people to buy things they don't want or need, then of course we will find it difficult to approach the whole concept of sales with a clean slate. This story of manipulation is often one we've inherited from family or friends who have been caught short or had a negative experience.

WHY SELLING IS THE MOST IMPORTANT THING

Over the years I've met hundreds of entrepreneurs who are passionate, talented, and have considerable expertise, but they also have major resistance to selling. These are the people who take course after course, get certification after certification, and have amazing plans about what they're going to do to change the world. I'm not being flippant and I don't mean to disrespect anyone; in truth it breaks my heart. You see this work is important and these people can help others. Their work is needed. And yet it will probably never get out into the world.

Without the ability to sell what you offer, your work is simply not viable as a business. Often these people will tell me they'll just hire a salesperson and get them to do the selling. But that doesn't work because if *you* can't sell what you do, then you can't hire anyone else to sell it for you. Before you can hire and train someone to sell for you, first you need to be able to create consistent sales.

So yes, you must learn to sell. There's no avoiding it. It's crucial to being able to build a business, no matter how large or small you envision it to be. If you want to build an empire, a huge business enterprise, you need to be able to sell. And if you want a small coaching practice, with just a few ongoing clients but a flow of those high-paying clients, then you need to be able to sell just the same.

But I don't think that's enough. We don't just want to learn how to sell; we can aspire to much, much more. And I don't think it's just about grinning and bearing it, or about slogging through and figuring it out.

You can learn to love selling. That might seem a little farfetched to you right now, but that's my goal. And I know it's achievable because I've done it and so have thousands of my clients. They've learned to embrace the story selling approach that dissolves your natural distaste or even disgust of selling and replaces it with curiosity, fascination, and even fun!

So that's our goal. Are you game? Let's do it!

A DIFFERENT KIND OF SELLING

My father used to go out early on a Sunday morning to buy fresh bagels and pop into the newsagent. He would bring home the weekend edition of the newspapers, the magazine my mother favored, and the various comics that each of us kids used to get. He would also bring home weekend treats. It was a tradition. I grew up reading these comics and magazines and I can see now how I was deeply affected by the images and stories that were sold to me.

Long before I was a teenager, I knew that I wasn't quite right. A little too tall with hair a little too wild, I was heavier than the stick-figure young girls represented in these publications. Like everyone in my generation, I was sold an impossible story about beauty and societal expectations.

And if that wasn't bad enough, along came social media to invite more comparison and outrageous, impossible expectations into the minds and hearts of us all. The story we are being sold, again and

Chapter 3: The Story of Selling

again, is that we aren't thin/fat/tall/short (or whatever physical attribute you want to add) enough; our skin color is not light enough or dark enough; we are not beautiful enough. And it doesn't end there. We are constantly being sold that we don't have enough, we're not smart enough, not innovative enough, not wealthy enough. In short, we are not enough.

After a while, we begin to believe it. It's exhausting. But it doesn't have to be that way.

Selling can be about something else entirely. Selling can be about your impact and your purpose. It's about identifying how you want to contribute to the world. To do positive, life-affirming, and supportive activities that will make the world a better place.

We need a revolution in our thinking about selling so that we begin to see our purpose expressed in the way we sell. So that we think of selling as the vehicle for growth and impact, where we can identify the difference between selling in your business and selling your soul. The first way to do that is to disconnect from the kind of selling that exhausts and drains you—the kind of selling that is devoid of integrity—and instead sell with the intention to love and take care of your potential client.

This different way of selling is fueled by our passion and our integrity. It's selling that speaks about transformation so that we and our clients are empowered to grow and contribute. It's a kind of selling we can connect to and get excited about.

Perhaps not surprisingly, it's a kind of selling that works extraordinarily well!

CHAPTER 4
Selling Through Story

"The story—from Rumpelstiltskin *to* War and Peace—*is one of the basic tools invented by the human mind for the purpose of understanding. There have been great societies that did not use the wheel, but there have been no societies that did not tell stories."*

—Ursula Le Guin, fantasy and science fiction author

IT WAS LATE. I was drinking my last cup of tea of the day and watching a TED Talk. A message came in from a local forum, looking for someone to work with their nonprofit to help a group of young women tell their story. I immediately wrote back, "Wow, this sounds like the perfect work for me. I'd love to learn more about what you do," and I included a link to my website.

Within minutes she responded. "You sound like the perfect fit for us! When can we meet?" We arranged to meet at a local coffee shop the next day.

The next morning, I took a brief look at their website. Then I went to the coffee shop to meet with the women who ran the organization. I asked them to tell me about what they do and what they need. They spent some time describing this incredible organization and the amazing coexistence work they do. I listened, fascinated by both their activities and the opportunity to contribute. Then I told them my story, all about the similar work I had done in the past and specifically about my passion for the very work they are committed to.

They asked a few questions, but I could tell by the glances that passed back and forth between them that they were excited. Then they asked if I would be available to join their group for a workshop just three days later. Yes, they hired me; it was that easy!

WHAT IS STORY SELLING?

It wasn't always that easy. In the past, I would discover an opportunity and then spend hours researching, trying to figure out exactly what they needed and how I could somehow show up exactly as that. I would twist myself into knots trying to figure out who I needed to be in order to be hired. It was stressful and very easy to lose sight of the fact that some opportunities were simply not right for me. I didn't realize that if I needed to become someone else to be accepted for a project, then perhaps it wasn't exactly the right thing for me. But I didn't really notice that because I was busy just trying to prepare to become the person they wanted.

This all changed when I discovered storytelling and realized that if I could tell a powerful story, that was enough. I realized that as long as my story is strong, one of two things will happen. Either they'll hear my story and realize that I'm right for them and they'll hire me, or the story will show them that the fit is not right. And that's perfect, because if I had tried to become what they wanted, no matter what I did or said, it would not have worked out. I might have gotten the job, but I would have been miserable, and it wouldn't have lasted. This way, using stories, I am relaxed and confident. I can communicate clearly and in a way that resonates with the clients who are perfect for me. Selling becomes easy and, yes, fun!

Story selling is about trusting in the power of storytelling to drive the selling experience. If you think about it, you'll see that this is not new. You've been influenced by stories to make purchasing decisions for years. As consumers, we have completely absorbed brand stories into our psyches, such as spending twice the amount to buy an Apple phone or computer because we essentially buy the story of the person we aspire to be—that is, the Apple user. Coca-Cola has been using storytelling for decades, telling us that the essence of connection, fun, and community contains the iconic bottle of Coke embedded in the experience.

We have been sold through stories since the beginning of time. It's now your turn to learn how to do it effectively, credibly, and with integrity in your business.

BRIDGING STORY TO SELLING

We sense the connection between the story and selling—we feel it, and we know it to be true. But why and how? Later we'll go into the details of how we create stories that sell, but first let's understand why it works.

Information versus Storytelling

Most people rely disproportionally on the power of information. Thus, when they compile data to create statistics, charts, and diagrams, they feel like they are armed with everything they need to make an impact, to get a decision, to enroll someone into their idea or their program. I saw this so often in my corporate career and then later as I began working with organizations all over the world. Managers and individual contributors alike take great pride and comfort in the impact of the information they hold in their hands. They fill their presentations with design features and credentials. They share objectives all laid out with details and promises, and they provide predictive outcomes. They suggest what is the likelihood of the strategy working.

The problem is that information only goes so far. And it's hard to predict or measure the impact the information actually has. Some people are swayed by information; many are not.

However, story is another thing. Storytelling is persuasive and the stories that people tell are what cause others to take action. It's based on the sharing of experiences, including the emotional shifts that take place when people take action and do the things that your service or program offers. This means that the results are clear, observable, and measurable. You see the immediate impact on people in the way they behave and how they feel.

In other words, storytelling is in a totally different realm from information and it's powerful because it moves us. We feel something and that feeling makes us take the next step.

It's not just about how we feel.

We Remember the Story

When we tell a compelling story, people tend to *remember* it. They are more likely to remember you and what you said because you've told a story.

Stanford professor Chip Heath conducted an interesting classroom experiment. Students were divided into groups and presented with statistics on crime patterns in the United States. Half the students argued that nonviolent crime is a serious problem, while the other half argued the opposite. After the presentations, students were asked to recall what they heard. Astoundingly, they discovered that students remembered 63 percent of the stories shared in the one-minute speeches, whereas only 5 percent of the statistics were recalled.

People are significantly more likely to recall stories than data.

Increasing Your Value

There are many examples of using storytelling to give a sense of the value of an item. From eBay listings to real estate home descriptions, when a story is told about a home or an item, its value skyrockets. I remember seeing an example of this when an elderly couple was selling their home. There seemed to be very little interest in their house, so they decided to try something new. They wrote a story about their home, the life they had lived there, the children they had raised, including the little accidents and the big celebrations that had occurred in the home. They described very personal details, such as the home improvements they had made when their daughter decided to get married in the house. Within two weeks of publishing the story of their home, they had several offers to buy it!

We Believe You; We Relate

When you tell an authentic story, we not only believe you, we find you relatable. When you share real stories with your audience, we get more of an insight into the type of person you are and can relate (or not!) to what you are doing and selling. If I hear someone telling a story from a perspective I can relate to, I believe in that person. It goes way beyond the story.

Know, Like, and Trust

The "know, like, and trust" factor is well described, but it happens much faster through story than any other means. When we tell a story about something that we care about, something that matters to us, the listener has the opportunity to see us in an authentic light. It offers a chance to get to know us at a deeper level and form a connection based on mutual beliefs or experience. When I tell a specific, real story about something I have gone through, the person hearing the story relates to the similar experience that they have lived through. The connection builds from this point.

Trust is one of the most important commodities in business and one of the hardest to earn. However, when you share a real story, trust develops almost instantaneously. We can't fake authenticity (though people try!) and so when we feel the real deal, we instinctively trust the story, and in turn trust the person telling it.

Trust is a crucial ingredient of sales success. When you can get your client to trust you, you can sell them pretty much anything!

USEFUL MODELS

There are some useful models when we think about the structure and flow of story, and how that may be applied to sales.

- **The Hero's Journey:** This classic storytelling model, popularized by Joseph Campbell, follows the hero on a transformative journey that starts with a call to adventure and goes through a cycle that includes challenges, mentors, and a triumphant return to home. When you use this model for selling, the customer is the hero, while the service provider can play the mentor guiding them to success.

- **Before and After Stories:** This is the sharing of real examples of how your service or program has transformed your client's life or business. You begin by sharing the struggle that one of your clients faced. There should be a moment of self-identification for your potential client, as they see their own struggle described. Then you share the outcome of the work you did with this former client and the amazing change it made for them. This is a very convincing type of sales story.

- **Problem to Solution Story:** This story focuses on what it was like before your work began—the problem that had challenged your ideal client. You create a clear picture of this scenario or "how the world is broken," and then engage your audience in the imagining of what it might look and feel like with a clear solution, which of course you can provide. The desire for the solution is the main driver of this story.

- **The Traditional Story Approach:** This is my personal favorite, though it's not always appropriate to use; you really have to read the room to make sure that this kind of story will resonate with your audience. Also, you need to be a good storyteller! This entails taking a folktale or fairy tale that has a hugely resonant message and sharing it as a metaphor for the opportunity that your listener or audience faces. Essentially these are the stories that I share in my podcast, *Once Upon a Business,* where I tell a traditional tale, and then share the implications and lessons relevant for business and entrepreneurs. Check it out.

- **Finding the New Bliss:** This is the terminology Nancy Duarte uses in her amazing book *Resonate: Present Visual Stories that Transform Audiences* (Wiley, 2010). Duarte researched successful presentations through the ages, from Martin Luther King Jr.'s "I have a dream" speech to Steve Jobs's presentation of the new Apple iPhone. She discovered patterns that emerged as key components for memorable presentations. Primarily she introduces the idea that great presentations are a form of storytelling, a narrative that engages and resonates with the audience. Sharing how stories can evoke emotions, create memorable moments, and drive action, she suggests that presentations, when cast as a story, are more impactful and memorable. One of the ideas that most "resonated" for me in this great book is how to structure your story for maximum impact. Duarte says that every presentation or story begins with establishing the norm, where we start from (what is), and moves towards the desired outcome (what could be). It's the movement between the two that helps define the gap between where you are and where you want to be. Ultimately the goal is to get to "the new bliss," where the idea has been accepted and a new norm created. When I really dug into this structure, I realized the massive impact of this for the sales process. Check out Duarte's TED Talk for more on this (https://www.ted.com/talks/nancy_duarte_the_secret_structure_of_great_talks).

STORY IN ACTION

The CEO sat across from me at his desk. I had spent the previous few minutes taking him through the proposal I had created based on what his HR director had told me they wanted—the same proposal he had already seen. Suddenly he pushed back from his desk, crossed his arms over his chest, and said, "This could be amazing and it could be rubbish. I'm just not sure which one it will be." I was speechless. The HR director sitting beside me, who had worked with me before, mumbled something about how she was sure it would be amazing, but I knew that my opportunity had just completely disappeared; the meeting was over.

The HR director managed to convince the CEO to meet me again the following week. I had realized my mistake and knew I needed a different approach. This time I was prepared. I started by asking him what their situation was right now, establishing the "what is" and then asked him questions to help him describe the "what could be" scenario. We went back and forth several times, which meant that he was beginning not only to see a clear picture of "the new bliss," but also to get a lot of clarity about the problems they were facing and what they needed to overcome in order to get to the desired outcome.

After a short meeting of about twenty minutes, he said, "Yes, let's do this. In fact, I'd like you to take the leadership team through a facilitated session to get more of this kind of clarity."

What a difference! I realized then, and many times later in similar situations, that you need to give your potential client clarity of their own story. First, they need to understand their current situation. Then they need to see the picture of their desired situation or goal, and what it will take to get them there. When you can give them the clarity of this story, they instinctively know that you're the person to take them on the journey. This is the power of this storytelling model for sales.

CHAPTER 5
Mistakes, Myths, and Untruths

"I thrive on obstacles. If I'm told that it can't be done, then I push harder."
—Issa Rae, actress, writer, and producer

IT WAS A MULTIPLE-DAY EVENT and the "guru" on the stage was energetic and dynamic. I had learned so much already. I met some interesting people out of the hundreds attending the event and I had been given great feedback about my budding business. I even had a new client from networking at the conference. I was thrilled; it was going to pay for the entire trip. I was feeling very optimistic about my new career path.

Just then the "guru" started talking about how to get clients into your business. He talked about understanding your audience, knowing their needs, and then he said, "Of course, you need to tell a powerful story." I waited with bated breath. And then he moved on. That was it. I couldn't believe it. Of course you need a powerful story, but how, when, where, what? I was stunned that he had just brushed over the very thing my entire business was about! But I also realized that this was a great opportunity, because though it's very simple, it's not always easy to create powerful stories for your business. There's a lot to learn.

Part of learning what to do in relation to telling stories for your business is to also know what mistakes to avoid and what *not* to do. Let's talk about the mistakes, myths, and untruths about storytelling for business. Here are some of the things that people say about storytelling for business:

- You have to be as vulnerable as you can.
- You must tell them everything about you.
- Every personal tragedy or challenge is material to tell for your business.
- People want to hear everything about you.
- Crying is an asset in your storytelling efforts.
- You can tell anyone's story and make it your own.
- If your story is true, it will always resonate with your audience.
- The more stories you tell, the more raving fans you'll have.
- You must have a signature story.
- You must use your signature story in everything you do in your business.

Sounds good, right? Well, no. These are actually ten myths about storytelling for business, and here's why:

1. *You have to be as vulnerable as you can.* Vulnerability can draw us in and help us find connection, but you should never be vulnerable for the sake of vulnerability. It can easily be inappropriate and uncomfortable. There are

few things worse than oversharing; it's never effective and often has the oppositive effect. Instead of bringing us closer it drives us away.

2. *You must tell them everything about you.* Though you find everything about you interesting, very few other people do! Most of what you know about you is inconsequential to the business interaction you hope to achieve with your potential client. You need to stick to what's relevant to the business and interesting or relevant to others.

3. *Every personal tragedy or challenge is material to tell for your business.* Your challenges and tragedies may be relevant to your business, but often they are not. More importantly, it can take time before you are able to understand your own challenges in a way that makes them interesting and relevant to your audience. If you are too close to the experience, it's not helpful to share it in a business context. You need to be super discerning about sharing your most intense inner pain.

4. *People want to hear everything about you.* What people really want is to hear everything about themselves. We are always focused on what we want and need, and if a story is relevant to that, then great. But they don't want to hear everything about you. You need to share in a way that helps them see themselves in your story. You want them to understand something about themselves that will motivate them to take action.

5. *Crying is an asset in your storytelling efforts.* Not always and usually not. Yes, it's a kind of vulnerability but you don't

want to make people feel that you are out of control, emotionally damaged, and unable to share appropriately. Also, you don't want people to feel that your interaction with them is part of your therapy. You need to help your audience feel the emotion without being overly impacted by the emotion yourself, in the moment.

6. *You can tell anyone's story and make it your own.* Your story belongs to you. Other people's stories belong to them. If you want to tell someone else's story, you need permission. If you do choose to share someone else's experience (with permission, if it's recognizable), you must do it in the context of why it's important to you or what it means to you. When you do this, it becomes your own story and will be impactful to your audience assuming it is relevant.

7. *If your story is true, it will always resonate with your audience.* Truth in storytelling is always subjective. What you remember and tell as a story is different to how someone else might tell the exact same experience (when my sister and I talk about our childhood and she recalls a situation that I was part of, I often find myself asking, Did we grow up in the same place? My version of the story is always different!) So not only is "truth" relative, it's also not criteria for resonance with your audience. Just because it's "true" does not make it interesting, relevant, or appropriate.

8. *The more stories you tell, the more raving fans you'll have.* Not necessarily. It's not about the quantity of stories, it's more about their authenticity and their relevance. You're better

Chapter 5: Mistakes, Myths, and Untruths

off telling one powerful, relevant story to your audience than constantly bombarding them with irrelevant anecdotes. This is part of the reason that I don't stay on people's mailing lists for very long; it starts being all about them, and that's not what I'm there for. I'm there to learn more about myself, so sometimes the sheer quantity of stories that don't hit the mark have the opposite effect of what was intended.

9. *You must have a signature story.* There's no such thing as a signature story—sorry to disappoint you! We have such a vast range of experiences throughout our lives, how can we possibly boil it down to one story? And why would we want to? I understand the concept that you should have one story that leads when you speak about what you do, but I just don't agree that one size fits all. We have many, many stories and we need to learn how to turn our experiences into compelling stories so we can tell them at the right time, in the right place, and to the right audience.

10. *You must use your signature story in everything you do in business.* Definitely not. There are many entrepreneurs out there, in the online space, who tell the same story, again and again. It's this story that seems to justify or give meaning to what they are doing, and so they tell it at every opportunity. But they end up telling it to death. Stories are vibrant, alive, ever-changing, and they should reflect the growing and changing presence you have in your business. Your stories are dynamic and should be compelling and audience focused. We need different stories for different parts of our business and activities in our business.

HOW TO DO IT WRONG!

There's no such thing as a "wrong" story. We can argue over factual accuracy or our memory of events. But basically stories, while completely subjective, exist in the realm of the storyteller's beliefs and decision about what they want to tell. However, telling stories for business can be done wrong. Aside from the "what-not-to-dos" listed above, there is one thing that's absolutely critical, that if you do it, you will be doing story wrong. Can you guess what it is? Okay, here you go.

Telling Stories to Manipulate, Mislead, or Lie to Your Audience

Historically, this was not uncommon. In fact, this is the reason that so many people distrust the idea of "story" for selling. When I was growing up in Ireland, it was not uncommon to hear people talk about "that person" who would sell their grandmother! The idea was that a person would sell anything to get what they want, no ethics, no values. Well, this is *not* what we're doing here.

Why This Is So Common

It's common to get storytelling wrong in all the ways I've spoken about because it's a bit like parenting. When you become a parent, there's an assumption that you'll just know what to do. When my first son was born, on the day I got to leave the hospital I couldn't believe they were giving this living person to me and assuming I'd know what to do. I remember a few weeks later, a nurse in the clinic telling me, "You know your child better than anyone. You'll understand what he needs." It was such a shock. I had no idea what I was supposed to do and wondered why they would trust me with this mammoth task. They don't send you to parenting school before the child is born; you just have to figure it out.

Well, with storytelling in business, many people assume that we'll just know how to do it. And occasionally you'll find people who are born naturals, like the people who are born with great timing and know how to tell jokes. But the majority of people are not like that. Most people need to learn how to find, craft, and tell stories. And that's great, because it's *totally* learnable (and that's what I'm here for!).

THE MYTHS OF STORYTELLING

When I first started Story Coach, I would go to business events and when people asked me "What do you do?" I would tell them that I'm a storyteller. Immediately, they would say, 'Oh, how lovely! So you work with children." I would respond, "No, never!" and then would need to explain all about storytelling for business. But this worked really well for me. If the purpose of networking events is to open a door or generate interest, this was a great conversation that did just that. People are always interested in hearing about something that seems to be different or not fit somehow.

Well, over the last fifteen years, that has changed. Most companies and entrepreneurs know the importance of having a good story for your product or service. The problem is that they don't always know what a story is, or how to use stories. I remember doing a workshop in a company that told me that storytelling was part of the vision and mission of the company, and yet they really didn't understand what that meant. We had a lot of work to do!

There are two major concerns about the use of storytelling, three myths that create confusion and concern. These myths of storytelling make it more challenging to master storytelling in business.

The first myth is the proliferation of fake news told as story. From politics to world affairs, from religion to culture, right across the board, it's getting more and more difficult to ascertain what is real and what is fake. Whether it's an image, a video, or a piece of text, it's fairly common to have a story passed around among thousands or even millions of people and assumed to be true, when it is actually fake. Aside from how terrifying it is, it makes it harder and harder to be authentic and to reach people.

The second myth concerns artificial intelligence. I'm not going to go into a rant about the danger and terror of the machines taking over, partly because who on earth knows what will happen, but mostly because I can see good uses of AI in relation to story. It's incredibly easy to ask ChatGPT or any other AI tool to create a story. Before you've had a chance to imagine anything of substance, you will get a flow of words that forms a story that's not bad, not bad at all, and it's taken only seconds to produce. But the myth is that this is enough! AI is an incredible way to avoid the blank screen, the pulsing cursor, and the lack of inspiration. It will get you going, start the ball rolling, and fill the page. That should not be mistaken for great storytelling—it's only the start.

The third myth is the idea that storytelling *is* the point. And this one I was seriously guilty of. When I started out in this business, I was so in love with the idea of teaching the world to be better storytellers. I believed that the story was the point! I just wanted to talk about the marvels and wonder of storytelling. I didn't realize at first that storytelling is the vehicle. You have a reason to communicate an idea. Maybe it's to influence or persuade someone to see your point of view. Maybe it's so you can enroll people into an idea or a program. Maybe it's to make the sale. It's not about the story you tell; it's about using storytelling as a vehicle to achieve all of the above.

Sales Gone Wrong

I almost don't need to tell you this. We all know what it feels like when sales go wrong. We are frustrated, disappointed, and full of doubt. You may be the very best coach, writer, project manager, or (fill in the blank), but if you don't know your worth and can't sell your service, you are just engaging in a hobby. And while hobbies are wonderful, they don't pay the rent!

And when you can't sell what you do, you start to doubt that you can do it at all. This doesn't make a lot of sense; just because you can't sell your services as a massage therapist doesn't mean you can't give a great massage. However, that's how we feel. When we don't manage to communicate how awesome we are at what we do and see that value reflected in a monetary exchange, it's very challenging to believe in ourselves. We simply forget how good we are.

Then there's another truth that we sometimes miss. It's actually much harder to sell something you don't believe in. It's more difficult to get behind an idea that doesn't ring true for you. And it's almost impossible to feel good about selling if you don't believe that what you are selling is good for the person who buys it. So there are some stages in the mastery of sales, and the story is what helps you move through these stages.

When you learn how to tell authentic, true stories about your expertise and your journey in your business, it not only impacts the potential buyer, it also reminds you of your abilities. The very act of telling a story in your business allows you to step into your brilliance and gain confidence about who you are and all that you do. Story is the ultimate tool of influence and persuasion, so you get great results too!

PART II

THE SEVEN-STORY FRAMEWORK

CHAPTER 6

Introduction to the Seven-Story Framework

"Stories are the way to capture the hopes, dreams, and visions of a culture. They are true as much as data are true. The truth of the powerful and irresistible story illustrates in a way data can't begin to capture. It's the stories that make you understand."

—Carl Sessions Stepp, professor, Philip Merrill College of Journalism

DURING MY CORPORATE CAREER as a learning and development manager, I always loved to get into the classroom. There's nothing quite like that moment when you see a spark in the learner's eye, when an adult gets to learn something new. It's thrilling. Whenever I could, I would design and deliver training, usually in the area of productivity, teamwork, and leadership development. I remember the day I was training a group of random people from across the organization on the subject of bullying and sexual harassment in the workplace. This is not a training course anyone really wants to take and yet, for compliance reasons, they all had to be there.

When we started out, people were uncomfortable, and we joked about how it was a "favorite" thing to learn about. As time went on, most people were reasonably engaged, though there was one person, Joe, who sat with his arms folded across his chest, leaning back on his chair, and refusing to say a word. Eventually Joe admitted that he thought this whole program was political correctness on steroids, and who needed it? Especially not decent people like himself.

That's when I paused, moved forward to perch on the edge of a desk so I was right in the middle of them all, and told this story:

> Early on in my career, I was the youngest person in the office I worked in. There was an older gentleman who I worked with and every time he spoke to me, he called me "dear." Sometimes he would gently touch my upper arm, occasionally if he came up behind me sitting at my desk, he would put his hands on my shoulders.
>
> I hated it. I felt sick from it. Though I knew he meant no harm, I was so uncomfortable I couldn't bear it. He reminded me of all the times men have hurt women (myself included). Though I knew he would have been horrified to know that I felt this way, and genuinely had no ill intent, I was stuck. What was I to do?

As I told the story, I noticed that Joe unfolded his arms and began to lean forward. As soon as I asked the question, he had an opinion; in fact, everyone did. There was more energy in that room after the story than there had been the entire day.

It was an amazing moment for me. Perhaps the first time I had ever truly experienced the power of storytelling in a business environment. From then on, the audience was engaged, the discussions animated, and everyone left at the end of the session thanking me, smiling and full of energy.

Chapter 6: Introduction to the Seven-Story Framework

Over the next few years, I experimented with telling stories in training sessions. I realized that the story makes the learning stick. It creates intense engagement and people not only learn more but retain more of the information from the training session. Yes, they enjoy the training and they remember more of what they learned so they can implement more. What an amazing shift took place in my sessions from that day on.

To be honest, when I left my corporate career and moved into creating a coaching business, I wasn't fully clear at first about what role storytelling would take.

My first take on storytelling was really about the coaching. I noticed that when we have experiences, we tend to tell other people about them—we tell them a story. And it's really interesting because there's very little objectivity in this story that we tell. We tell a story that is mostly what we remember or the impression we have about what happened. It's influenced by prior experiences, our education, and our expectations. So when we tell other people "what happened," essentially we are telling a story that is about 95 percent made up.

The problem is that we forget that we've made up the story and we consider it the truth. This works fine if it's a story that empowers us, a story that works well. But when the story diminishes us, or disempowers us, we are equally committed to it as "truth" and we continue to live by this story.

What I noticed was that if you change the story, you change your reality, and that's very exciting. So, as a coach, if I can help people to identify, understand, and change their story, they can change their reality and meet their expectations and desires for what they want in their lives. This concept, developed over many years, became Story Coaching (including the Certified Story Coach program, among others).

However, in the process of creating training programs and coaching people to this new methodology I call "story coaching," I noticed that coaches particularly are generally really bad at talking about their business in a compelling way.

Like many business owners, coaches fall in love with what they do. When they try to market their business, they tend to talk about the process that they love so much. And yes, they love it because it works, but as I love to tell coaches, nobody wants coaching. They want the results that coaching can deliver. So as coaches speak about their process, the potential client goes cold. But if they speak about the result they can help them achieve, they become interested and even excited about working together.

I find it heartbreaking. I love coaches. I love the passion they bring to their work and their desire to make the world a better place. And yet so many of them coach as a hobby because they can't make a living out of it. That's wrong. And it doesn't have to be that way.

So I started looking into helping coaches learn how to tell compelling stories so that they can attract clients and build a business—a real business, not just a hobby. Over the next decade and more, I discovered that there are certain stories that make *all* the difference in your business. If you don't have these stories clear and ready, you are at a real disadvantage because you just can't attract quality clients at the rate you need to build a viable business.

The next step was to build out a story framework to help coaches and entrepreneurs, like you, discover the most important stories that you need to make your business a success.

THE IMPORTANCE OF THE FRAMEWORK

It's not just a random story here and there. And it's certainly not the same story used again and again ad nauseum, until everyone is sick of hearing it and doesn't even believe it anymore.

I remember hearing one of these coach "gurus" tell me his story for the first time. It was a pretty impressive story about a car crash he had had in his early twenties. He explained how he nearly died and found himself wondering if he had lived a good life, if he had made a difference. Once he recovered, those questions never left him, and it set him on a path to find meaning and to make an impact in the world. Cool story, right?

Well, yes and no. He told that story before every webinar, at every live event, and in his sales copy. I had to wonder if anything else important or interesting had happened to him, and after a few years I began to wonder if the story was even true.

The trick is not just to find your one single story, the one that set you on this path, but instead to learn how to find, craft, and tell stories right across your business so that you can have maximum impact on your prospective audience.

This resulted in the framework I developed and the "Seven Stories that Sell." You may wonder whether there are more, and yes, there are more stories that can and should be told in your business. But these seven are the critical ones, the stories that will help you catapult your business into more profitability, more clients, and more fun!

THE SEVEN STORIES THAT SELL

The Story of You

- The "Here's who I am" story—the story that makes an immediate impression.
- This is your "impact" story.

The Story of What

- The story that answers "What happened to you?"
- What was that pivotal experience that made you realize that this is what you need to be doing in your life and in your work?
- It's your business's "origin story."

The Story of Who

- The story that explores "Who is your work for?"
- Who would be most impacted by what you offer?
- Who does this affect?
- Who is your customer?

The Experience Story

- The "What happened" story, where you share the powerful moments of lived experience that describe what happened to you that made this journey so impactful.
- When you share this, your audience understands that this could happen to them too.

- It establishes the possibility of transformation from your work.

The Failure Story

- The story of when things went very wrong—the pain, the shame, the vulnerability.
- It's where your humanity shows up.
- It's always accompanied by how you picked yourself up, brushed yourself off, and started all over again.

The Vision Story

- The story that describes the desired future for yourself and your business, and the reader or listener can also envision it for themselves.

The Proof Story

- The stories told by you in the form of client experiences or stories told by clients in the form of testimonials.
- It's the proof that your service or program works, that it gets results.
- It's the voice of the people who have been impacted by your work.

Before we dive into each of the seven stories in-depth, and learn how to craft them, we need to understand where the story comes from. What are the seeds of great stories?

The answer is simple: it's the *pivotal moment*.

PIVOTAL MOMENTS

We all have events in our lives that change everything. These are the times when something big happens. It is the birth of a child or the death of a loved one. It is an unexpected diagnosis or the miraculous recovery from an illness. It is moving house, or country. It is changing your job or your career. These are the huge life events that give us a new perspective, and life never quite feels the same again. The meaningful life events may make for interesting stories, but what is more poignant are the single points in time, the smaller instances where something shifts. Story happens in a single moment in time. These are pivotal moments that occur within the larger events, and also in ordinary day-to-day life. They are the quiet moments where, either in real time or in retrospect, we are not quite the same after as we were before. And these "pivotal moments" happen all the time, sometimes several times a day!

Usually, we recognize a pivotal moment because it makes us feel something, and it's unexpected. It may be a shift to something more positive or something more negative; the point is that we are moved, and we recognize it because of how we feel. Another way we recognize a pivotal moment is by a shift in the way we think. We may have understood something one way and now, since this moment, we begin to see it in a different light. There is a shift in our thought process. There are also big shifts that touch on our belief system; something happens that affects us so deeply that we may question what we actually believe about the world or a certain situation. Sometimes it's a shift that really challenges us personally—this usually points to something we were believing about ourselves that no longer feels true. On other occasions, it can relate to our environment, a job, or a relationship, and the

Chapter 6: Introduction to the Seven-Story Framework

assumptions we hold about them may be seriously questioned. When you start paying attention to these shifts and what motivates them, you will notice that they occur all the time and they are usually story worthy. They are the starting points for crafting stories.

Pivotal moments are not only in the big events in life. They happen all the time, every day. And in your business, they are all around you. Pivotal moments are the seedlings of great story. When you feel something, notice it. Write down what happened—literally, step-by-step, what happened. That's where we start, by remembering a meaningful moment and then crafting it into a compelling story for our business.

When I started my business, my business coach told me that if I wanted to build an audience, I needed to tell a story every week in my newsletter. At that time I was sending out a newsletter once every month. When she told me this, I laughed. "My life is not that interesting," I said. "Where will I find a story *every week?*"

She replied, "I trust you, you'll find the stories." So from that day on, for the next ten years, I found a story that I would write and send out to my growing list every Tuesday. I would notice or remember something—what I later came to call the pivotal moment—and then I would write about it. Some of these moments connected to the seven stories that sell, others less so.

But I started to see a structure for story and a use for it. All this added up to that precious moment where I sat down to identify these seven most important stories, and to begin the thought process that would ultimately lead to writing this book.

Alright, it's time to get started with the seven stories. Sit tight—here we go!

CHAPTER 7
The Story of You

"Great stories happen to those who can tell them."
—IRA GLASS, radio host and producer

THE STORY OF YOU is what you say about you, the first thing that pops out of your mouth when you have a chance to introduce yourself. It sums up "Here's who I am" and should make an initial impression that will last and be memorable.

WHAT IS THIS STORY?

The truth is that many people get this story wrong in relation to their business. They either stutter and stumble without quite knowing what to say so we're left confused and unimpressed, or they learn a formula by heart that someone has recommended to them and then share it in the most inauthentic way. These tend to be the most common responses to the questions "Who are you?" or "What do you do?"

Here's the thing, though. We get the opportunity to talk to people many times every day. Whether it's a formal meeting at a networking event or just a chance meeting on a train, people will often ask you what you are up to, what you do. So it's incredibly important to be able to answer these questions easily, in a relaxed manner, and at the same time to make a great impression so that the person not only likes what you say, but also wants to know more. If the Story of You is working, it means that people will walk away remembering not only what you said, but how you made them feel.

THE FORMULA

There is a simple formula for the Story of You.

Part 1

You start with a statement about your passion: what you truly care about.

- Remember, you don't care about the process you are sharing or teaching; you care about the outcome. And I don't use the word "passion" lightly; you need to home in to what really drives you, what wakes you up at night, what you would do even if you were never paid for it. What is it that you feel you have a genuine talent for and that you do easily, so much so that you wonder why everyone else doesn't do it? What is it that makes you want to jump out of bed in the morning and you forget or lose time when you're deeply involved in it?

Part 2

Add the story about what happened that made you aware why this is important.

- Something happened to you, or perhaps many things happened around this topic that you can call on to share this moment. But there was at least one moment when you realized, "This passion of mine, it's important, it means something and not just to me. And if I share this moment with others, it will impact them in a positive way." This story may be from a long time ago, before you thought about creating your business; it's the moment that you knew you were onto something, and you were ready to explore what this might mean.

Part 3

Sum up with a clear statement of who you serve, what they experience, and how you offer transformation.

- This is a formula you may be more familiar with. It follows an easy flow describing who you work with (your ideal client), what they struggle with, how you help them, and what they can expect when they work with you. This is the sentence you can really work on; just be careful not to make it sound too practiced and therefore inauthentic. It's okay to change this sentence around to try it out and find the one that fits best.

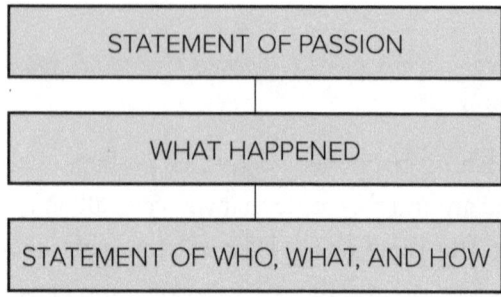

Some Examples of the Story of You

I'd like to share with you a few examples of this story type. I'll present the short version, which is the one you might use when you meet someone for the first time. It's the door opener, the way to get someone's attention, and the whole point of the short version is for the listener to say, "Tell me more!" The slightly longer, more in-depth version is for when you know a person already—you have gauged their interest, and it tells you that they want to learn more.

Lisa's Story

THE SHORT, COMPELLING VERSION: I'm passionate about the power of storytelling. I remember that, as a corporate trainer, I saw the transformation in my students when I told a story. There was amazing engagement and connection—that's when I knew I was onto something. So now I support entrepreneurs to attract clients and build their business with the power of storytelling.

THE LONGER, MORE IN-DEPTH VERSION: I've always been interested in stories. Since I was a little child, I would ask my parents and grandparents to tell me their childhood stories. I was super curious. As a professional trainer, I came across storytelling unexpectedly. As a trainer, you need to facilitate classes on all kinds of topics, some of which you may not find terribly interesting. I discovered that I would tell stories to try to bring more life and interest into the classroom, to amuse myself first (to be honest) and others! That's when I noticed that when I told stories, something very interesting happened that I didn't expect. People started paying more attention to the topic; they were really leaning in and began to engage in a totally different way. There was more conversion, more interaction, and by the time the session was finished, I saw that there was more learning too. In the days and weeks after each training session I saw that when I told stories, there was more retention of the learning achieved in the training sessions. I could see that storytelling was magic. So when I started my business, I realized that if I could tell a good story about what I do, then I would have an advantage in the marketing of my services. When I started working with coaches, I saw that they really struggled to talk about what they do in a compelling way and that so many coaches don't have nearly enough clients. That's when I decided to help coaches and other entrepreneurs to tell their stories so they can attract clients and sell their services.

Jeff's Story

THE SHORT, COMPELLING VERSION: I'm passionate about mentoring teens. I was viciously bullied, and I don't know where I would have ended up if I didn't have an older cousin who took an interest and helped me find myself again. So I've dedicated my life and my business to providing a support network to kids who are suffering.

THE LONGER, MORE IN-DEPTH VERSION: I still shudder when I remember the kids who bullied me in the school playground. The break in classes was supposed to be a time to relax, run around, get refreshed from the outdoors, but I dreaded it. I knew that just as soon as I would breathe in the cool air, someone would say something mean. I would be tripped up, pushed over, and thumped in places where the bruises would not be seen. I became withdrawn and very jumpy. I was very, very unhappy.

My cousin was two years older than me, and we went to the same school. He was a popular kid, very athletic and liked by everyone. I adored him and we had a great connection. He was the only person in my family who noticed the change in me over that year. When I refused to tell him much, he began to pay attention in school and eventually saw what was going on. He reached out to my parents, my teachers, and to the bullies themselves. It made all the difference. But it took years for me to get back my confidence and get strong again. After years in a dull job, I realized that I needed to do something related to my experience. I'm passionate about helping kids get through this, quicker and more easily than I did. So I work with families, schools, and the kids themselves so they can beat their bully and heal.

Sharon's Story

I knew that my marriage was a mistake just after my son was born. We separated immediately and the same day that the divorce was finalized, I met Simon. His wife had passed away the year before and he was left alone with their two young kids. There was an immediate connection. We were married before the year was out! It took a while for the kids to adjust and then we decided we wanted kids together,

Chapter 7: The Story of You

so we had two more. Now we have a blended family with five kids. I wanted to learn everything I could about being a parent of all these kids with different backgrounds and different needs. I discovered an amazing world in parenting classes, and it became my passion. When my kids got a bit older I became a Certified Parenting Coach and now I work with parents of blended families to help them create happy, integrated, and secure kids who feel loved while their parents thrive too.

WHAT TO EXPECT

When you have a powerful Story of You, you can expect a change in how you feel about the work you do and your confidence to talk about it. This story is a powerful reminder of who you are and what led you to the work you are so passionate about. This means that you get a burst of energy when you tell this story and that feels great! You are reminded that it's not by chance that you are doing what you do. You are immensely connected and qualified to be serving in this area. You are in the right place.

As for the people who hear you tell this story, they will remember who you are and what you do, long after you have met. When you tell the Story of You, well, you can expect to be engaged in a longer conversation and if there's a fit, it's likely that they'll want to work with you.

Here's the template of the Story of You so you can get started!

The Formula

Start with a statement about your passion. Then you add the story about what happened to you that gave you the awareness of why this is important. And finally, you sum up with a clear statement of who you serve, what they experience, and how you offer transformation.

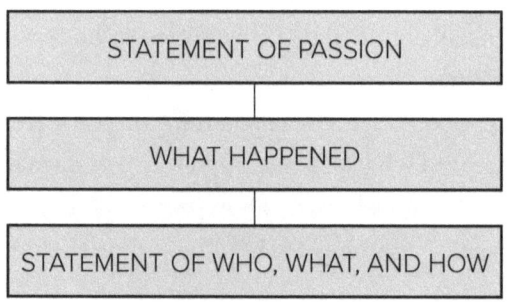

Chapter 7: The Story of You

I am passionate about _____

_____

It was [time/place/defining event] _____

_____**when [x happened].**

I noticed [what you see] _____

_____

I felt _____

_____

Then I knew I was onto something.

So now, I support [x—who] are experiencing [y—what] and help them [z—the "how" that delivers the outcome].

_____

_____

CHAPTER 8

The Story of What

*"Storytelling is our obligation to the next generation.
Give something of meaning to your audience by engaging and educating them.
Stop marketing. Start storytelling."*

—LAURA HOLLOWAY, health and wellness expert

THE STORY OF WHAT answers the question of what happened to you. Or more correctly, what happened for you! This is when you believe, as I do, that things never happen *to* us exactly but instead they are the events that shape us, that inform us, and that are ultimately there to help us grow and learn.

WHAT IS THIS STORY?

We all have formative experiences that have a big impact on us, whether it's the death of a loved one, moving to a new town, changing schools, or perhaps later in life it's the toxic work environment that changes our professional path or the mentor/teacher who inspired us to learn something completely unexpected. These events mark us and change us, and we carry them with us forever, sometimes without even realizing.

When something important happens in our lives, it's an invitation to look closely and see the lesson it has provided for us. As we know, there is nothing new under the sun and stories are universal, so as you share the event that shaped you, chances are the person listening to this story has had an experience not unlike it. So we connect through the story. Even though the "what" might be quite different, we have experienced the emotion around the event in something that is similar enough for us to relate. This is how the Story of What can resonate so deeply.

WHY SHOULD WE TELL IT?

When you are creating a business that matters to you, it's not just a way to make money. There is a compelling reason why you have come to this profession, and it's informed by events like the Story of What. This is usually a very compelling story that not only shares the reason you came to your understanding of the topic, but also speaks to what you deeply believe. So in describing the experience, this fascinating story illustrates what you truly stand for. It is a clear indication of your values and what you believe in. This is what connects you to your audience. When you take a stand, it might alienate people who don't believe in the same things as you, but that's fine; they are not your target audience. At the same time, it draws in the people who do believe in what you stand for and what is so meaningful for you and them too.

When you share your Story of What, it builds your credibility because it explains how you have this passion and drive towards your topic and therefore have built your expertise. Sometimes the Story of What has a fairy-tale quality to it because it often comes from way back in your past. It has not only made a significant mark on you and has driven your passion, it also has become a huge motivator for you. The Story of What that your audience can deeply relate to becomes a motivator for them too.

THE FORMULA

There is a simple formula for the Story of What.

Part 1
Way back when (time and place)

- We start by going back to a long time ago, perhaps far, far away. As with all stories, they only ever happen in a specific moment of time, so you need to describe that time and the place. The more details that ground us in that time and place, the more the story will come alive. Don't be afraid to place us exactly where the story began; this is what makes us see and feel what happened. And simply tell what occurred. The biggest mistake people make when they try to tell a story is that they get caught up in what it all meant, without actually sharing what exactly happened. So tell us where you are, when it was, and what happened.

Part 2
Why it was a surprise

- The only reason that this event is interesting, both to you and to your audience, is because it was unexpected. We have certain assumptions about how the world works, how people behave, and what's going to happen, and then there is a surprise and it's not at all as we expected. This is the core of interesting stories. So share why this was unexpected and what was the surprise. Remember, this is your world, so don't worry about whether other people may have anticipated what was going to happen; you didn't and that's all that matters. Share your perspective so that it's clear what surprised you.

Part 3
How it made you feel

- Sometimes we assume that others know what we feel and that we don't have to explain or share that. I can tell you from bitter experience that this is not the case! I'm guilty of this, assuming by sharing what happened that others will understand how surprising or joyful or devastating it all was for me. Well, that doesn't work; you need to share how this event made you feel. Remember, you don't have to tell them the actual emotion; you can describe what happened to you. For example, instead of saying, "I was terrified," you can say, "My knees were shaking, and I thought I might faint from fear." Remember, you can show rather than tell, which is often a more effective approach to storytelling.

Part 4
What you knew you had to do

- Finally, this story was what informed your decision to begin to work in the area of your expertise, so share this. As a result of what happened, you made certain decisions in that moment, or perhaps later. Maybe this incident planted a seed, so describe what that was. Sometimes it's only in reflection that we realize the implication of the events we witness or experience. And so you simply share that later, upon reflection, you realized what it all means to you.

Remember, the story of what always contains a certain urgency. This is because it became such a powerful driver towards the direction you ended up pursuing. So don't be afraid or forget to describe that urgency. This should be a pretty passionate story!

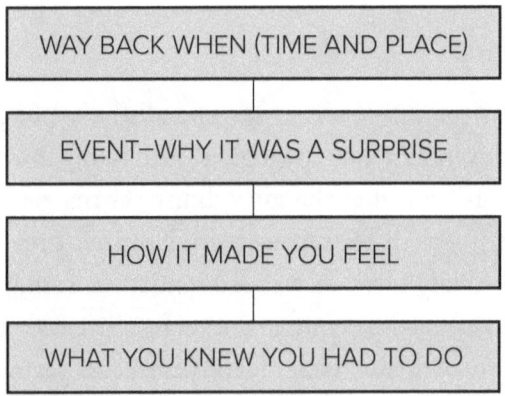

Some Examples of the Story of What

Lisa's Story

It was difficult to get out of the house in the evenings during this time. My kids were small and often sick, and my partner was traveling most of the time. Somehow I was able to arrange a sitter that night. I was invited to a storytelling evening and though it sounded interesting, I wasn't sure what to expect. I walked into the crowded hall where the storytellers were already on the stage. As they began to share their stories I had a visceral feeling of connection. My senses were heightened. I felt a tightening in my stomach and intense excitement. It was almost as if the walls were vibrating, I felt so alive and I realized that this is what I'd been doing my whole life; I just didn't know what it was called. As a trainer, I had been telling stories. In my personal life, I was always telling stories. I knew in that moment that I had to learn more, and that I wanted to become a professional storyteller. Much later, I realized that I didn't want to be an entertainer; I wanted to help others learn how to tell powerful stories too.

Judy's Story

As a young lawyer, I thought I was like all the other guys who also graduated and were hired by the biggest firm in my town. That is, until I got married. It's not that the guys didn't get married too; they did. But somehow it was different for them. Not that I realized it at first. Then it was brutally clear. It was a Monday morning; I had arrived early because I needed to complete a report that was due by 10 a.m. I was at the copy machine when I overheard two partners in the next room talking about "the newbies." They were discussing all about who they thought had potential and who didn't. When my name came up, there was a laugh. "Well, we can forget her, she'll be having babies soon enough—no serious future there." I was stunned and horrified. I couldn't believe that these attitudes still existed, which was more typical of the era when my mother had to leave her job because she got married. Ever since that day, I've been committed to creating equal and diverse workplaces where no one has to ever feel discriminated against.

Jason's Story

I had been struggling with a sports injury for years. I would get some relief but inevitably the pain would return, and nothing seemed to help. It was my right shoulder, and I was so fed up with it. Then one day my friend suggested I try working with an osteopath; she knew someone good. I'd tried everything, so why not. The osteopath began to massage and manipulate my head, neck, and then my shoulders. Right away it felt different, I got immediate relief and it continued to feel better. After a few months, I was so impressed with the sessions and how I felt that I got really interested in why this worked when other things hadn't. That was it; I decided to study the field and it took a few years, but I got trained and now I work with sports injuries, and I love it. I'm so happy that I can help people who've tried everything but are still experiencing pain. I know I can help them recover fully and lead an active life again.

WHAT TO EXPECT

The opportunity of the Story of What is that it helps you create great allies and followers in your work. When a person hears this story and relates to your experience, they immediately recognize that your passion and drive is important to them too. What happens is that you attract like-minded prospects who are similarly driven. The difference is that they are way behind you in their journey and they need your guidance. They want to work with someone who has had the experience way back when. They want to be inspired by someone who has built the knowledge and expertise that will help them figure out their own path. The Story of What becomes a magnet for your very best clients because they have the passion for what you deeply care about, and they are also willing to take a stand.

Here's the template of the Story of What so you can get started!

The Formula

The formula for the Story of What starts by taking us back to a long time ago, perhaps far, far away. Start by bringing your listener or reader back to that time and place. Share the specific moment of the event, what happened, and why it was so surprising. Finally, you must share how it made you feel and what you had to do as a result. There is always an urgency in the Story of What, because it became such a powerful driver.

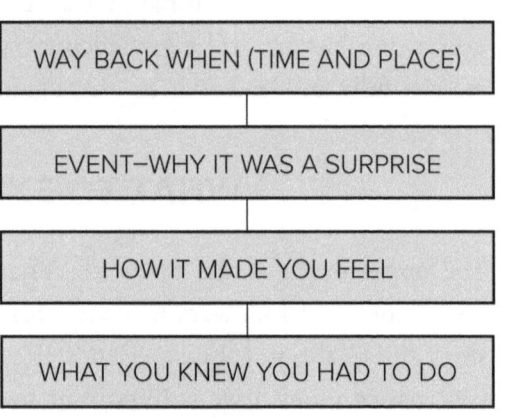

Chapter 8: The Story of What

It was _____

_____

[details of time and place and the specific event].

The reason it was so unexpected was that _____

_____

I felt _____

_____

And I knew that I had to _____

_____

CHAPTER 9
The Story of Who

> *"Stories create community, enable us to see through the eyes of other people, and open us to the claims of others."*
>
> —PETER FORBES, educator, writer, and facilitator

THE STORY OF WHO explores who your work is designed for. It is the story that will draw in the person who would be most impacted by what you offer. This is the story that as you craft it, you begin to consider things like who your work most affects, who your perfect client is, and who the customer is who will be most satisfied by your work.

WHAT IS THIS STORY?

In many cases people focus on the work itself, the process, the transformation, and the outcomes, without considering who is the target customer. This is a huge mistake because it becomes impossible to attract clients if you're not clear who your client actually is. The other scenario is when we feel that our work is needed by everyone.

I used to do my work in a local coffee shop years ago. I would find my usual spot and say hi to the regulars who also brought their work there. The marketing director in a hi-tech company, the university lecturer, the student of medicine, the software engineer, and the teacher all had their regular spots too. Every time I was asked what I do and I would explain about the power of storytelling for business, they would inevitably tell me that my work was so badly needed in their field. They would suggest that it would be a great business opportunity for me to work with the university or the hospital or the school. And they may have been right, but I knew that though I could have worked with all of them, it wouldn't have helped me grow my business. I needed to home in on and define my client so that I could tell the right stories that would make sense to them, attract them in, and actually build my business. So if you're one of those people convinced that your work is needed everywhere and by everyone, you may be correct. But unless you are willing to home in on and work with one audience at a time, it will be very difficult to be successful in building your business. You must start by figuring out your very own Story of Who!

WHY SHOULD WE TELL IT?

The most important reason you need to tell a clear and well-defined Story of Who is so that your ideal clients can recognize themselves in your story and self-select for your programs or services. When a person hears a story and sees themselves in it, they realize that the person telling the story understands them and has insight into their very specific situation. They hear that you have had relevant experience and that you care about the issues that are most important to them. This means that your ideal client can easily determine that you are the perfect person to provide a service specifically tailored to them.

When you create your Story of Who, you are essentially drawing in your ideal client. What is the ideal client? It's the kind of client you feel energized by working with. You know that you can help them, give them a ton of value, and support them in their transformation to achieve what they most desire. That's a powerful experience and quite the opposite from the kind of client that you find exhausting, exasperating, and hard to help. These are the clients we sometimes call "uncoachable" but in fact it's often simply a mismatch between the coach and the client. Instead, when you find and tell your Story of Who, then it becomes easy to identify who you should be working with.

To prepare to craft and tell the Story of Who, you need to thoroughly understand your ideal client. That means you really have to get into their heads and see the world through their eyes. You should be able to identify the biggest challenge that they face, the reasons they wake up at night in a sweat and can't get back to sleep. And you need to understand their greatest desire. The best way to get this level of understanding is to make sure that you are constantly talking to the people you think are your ideal clients so that you understand them better and better. Researching your target audience by talking to them is the very best way to do this. Always and forever be talking to your target clients, which tells you all you need to know about them so you can target your offers, your marketing, and your stories.

THE FORMULA

Part 1
The client

- The formula for the Story of Who begins with a description of the ideal client that is simple, clear, and specific. You need to present a clear picture of what they look like and then describe them in a place that would be typical for them, doing something quite normal. We need to get a basic sense of who these people are, what they care about, and how they tend to behave.

Part 2
Their frustration or pain

- The next step in the Story of Who is to describe their frustration or pain in doing something that is a critical part not just of their life in general but of their day-to-day world. This needs to be a pain or frustration that's not mild or by-the-way; it's something that prevents them from doing or being what they want. Typically, this "pain" will prevent them from living the life they want and has been going on for quite some time. They have tried to resolve this frustration in other ways but have not been successful.

Part 3
The possibility

- The third part of the Story of Who is to show the possibility for this person: first that it is possible to find a resolution to the problem they are facing, and that many others have been able to resolve this pain or frustration. Next is to help them understand that it's not just possible in general but it's possible for them too. This is the promise of what could be when they get your help.

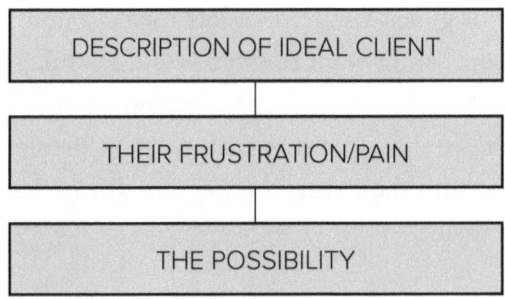

Here are some examples of the Story of Who

Lisa's Story

I loved meeting people at the coaching conferences I went to. Over the years of attending, I began to notice that the people I met were very distinctive. They were passionate, mission-driven folk who wanted to make the world a better place. I would love to hear them talk, listen to them describe their ideals and their plans, and hear the passion and drive in their voices.

Just after lunch at one of these events, a stylish young woman sat down beside me. We started to chat and I asked her, "What do you do?" With a sigh in her voice and no conviction whatsoever, she said, "I'm a coach. I help people find transformation." I did my best to hold back and not sigh out loud too. I had heard this kind of statement so many times over the three days of the conference.

It told me nothing and did no justice to this really lovely woman. I asked myself yet again, Why were coaches so bad at telling their story? Almost every coach in that place (and there were thousands there) was saying more or less the same thing. It told me nothing about who she was and what she did, never mind why I should hire her. This kind of general statement left me cold and frustrated. You see, I love coaches and I want them to be successful in their amazing missions, but I knew that this kind of introduction or statement did nothing to achieve that. It was in that moment I realized that I need to help coaches find their story so they can attract clients and make their business thrive!

Marc's Story

Marc is a marriage counselor who shared about his client, let's call her Susy. "Susy heard about me through a mutual friend. She had been married for more than twenty years, had three kids, and was at her wit's end. She and her partner had been estranged for months. At first it was just the occasional argument, but it seemed to get worse and worse over the years. Now it was her oldest son's graduation from high school. She didn't know how she could continue the facade for the kids that everything was okay when she felt her life was falling apart. She was sick and tired of being sick and tired and she couldn't see a way out. At first her husband didn't want to come to therapy, so she came to see me alone. It only took a few weeks for her to get a lot of clarity about what she needed and what was going wrong between them. Soon her partner noticed that she seemed to be doing much better and agreed to try too. They began to attend sessions together. They worked hard to figure out how they could be better together in every way. When their second child reached her graduation, there was no facade to keep up—they were doing really well!"

Susana's Story

They say I could swim before I could walk. I'm happiest in the water. It became more serious in high school when I joined the swim team and we practiced for hours every day. I progressed into competitive swimming, both individually and in teams. I just loved it! I'll never forget Jessie on our team, who was the strongest swimmer by far; she was like a fish. But just when we were about to win the championship, she pulled out. It was from one day to the next, she just didn't show up. Our coach said she was sick but there seemed to be some mystery about it all. Later we found out that she had been suffering from anxiety; she'd had a total breakdown and was unable to swim anymore. I was stunned. I couldn't stop thinking about how she must have been struggling for a long time but hadn't shared it with anyone. I knew I would go into a profession relating to sport and quickly I realized that I wanted to help young athletes cope with the mental stress around performance. Jessie's situation could have been avoided. So now I help young athletes strengthen their mental game so they can avoid anxiety and burnout and continue to enjoy their sport.

WHAT TO EXPECT

When you have a strong Story of Who, you will see that you are attracting ideal clients, the kind of people you love to work with. I've sometimes had clients so awesome that I wonder why they're paying me. I'm having so much fun and it's so empowering for me too, it feels like it's not even close to work! With a clearly defined

Story of Who, you'll see that the people who speak to you about working with you are so totally aligned with you and your approach that almost everyone you speak to will agree to work with you. Your close rates for sales conversations will increase meaningfully. This is because it is so much easier to sell to someone who has already self-selected. Before they even speak to you, they are quite convinced that you are the person they want to work with. It becomes your choice as to whether you want to work with them.

I remember when I started my business, I would work with anyone who was even vaguely interesting or interested in working with me. That resulted in working with clients who were exhausting and not terribly aligned with what I was interested in. If I'm being really honest, it also meant that I was probably less able to support them in achieving what they most desired. There just wasn't the alignment that I've come to see is possible. Once I discovered the power of the Story of Who, it meant I get to choose to work with the most wonderful people who are an absolute pleasure to serve and with whom I get the very best results!

Here's the template of the Story of Who so you can get started!

Chapter 9: The Story of Who

The Formula

The formula for the Story of Who begins with a description of the ideal client that is simple, clear, and specific and places them in a typical place doing something quite normal.

Then you must describe their frustration or pain in doing something that is a critical part of their day-to-day activity. The story will conclude when you have shown the possibility for this person and the promise of what is possible when they get your help.

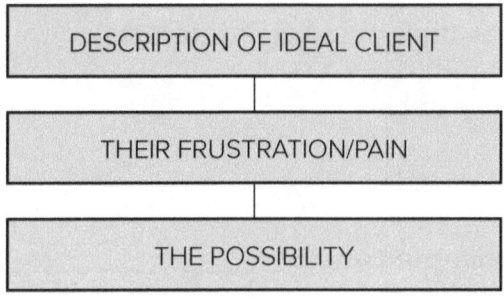

`I'm passionate about _____

_____

[describe your ideal client].

They deeply care about _____

_____

[what defines their passion or interests].

They are concerned about _____

_____

[what worries them].

Describe a specific time and place when you were in contact with this client _____

_____

Chapter 9: The Story of Who

I noticed that _____

_____

[What did they say/do?].

I felt _____

_____

[What moved you and why?].

I understood that _____

_____

[What did you understand as a result?].

It changed how I _____

_____

[think, what I do, the kind of work I follow, etc.].

CHAPTER 10

The Experience Story

"Marketing is no longer about the stuff that you make, but about the stories you tell."

—SETH GODIN, author and entrepreneur

THE EXPERIENCE STORY shares an important incident in your life. It's where you describe the powerful moments of lived experience that happened to you and that moved you towards the work you feel called to do. It is the start of the impactful journey that led to where you are right now in your business.

WHAT IS THIS STORY?

Generally, we want to point to an early experience that put us on our particular path, rather than a more recent experience that may confirm our commitment to the cause or subject we are working with. The experience story recalls an important moment in our life, a time where something we experienced changed our trajectory in life and then later in business.

By sharing this experience, your audience understands that you are genuine and credible. This is also a wonderful reminder for you of the authentic experience that you bring to your work. By hearing your experience, the audience instinctively understands that this could happen to them too, if it hasn't already. The experience story speaks to your own personal transformation and therefore establishes the possibility of the transformation available to your clients from working with you.

WHY SHOULD WE TELL IT?

The experience story is the starting point for the journey you've been on while creating your business. It adds depth and insight to the credibility that you bring. The successful experience story is usually very relatable to your ideal client. So this is the story that makes your prospect think, Well if she can do this, why can't I? It answers the concern that we all have that maybe this is a great service for someone else, but will it work for me? The experience story needs to be carefully chosen so that it doesn't feel out of reach for the listener. Instead, the experience story describes a normal situation, something that is familiar and recognizable to the audience, but then something unexpected happens. This is the essence of compelling story, the surprise, the moment when the unexpected catches us and the previous "normal" spins away out of reach. However, despite this surprise, your story will show how you have overcome the unexpected event, the challenge. It will illustrate how you have managed to go beyond it.

Sometimes we have unusual experiences in life that seem clearly disconnected from the work we do. Over the years I've seen that some of the most unexpected experiences are, in fact, deeply connected to the passion we feel about the work we do (assuming we are actually doing work that's meaningful and heart centered). I have come to believe that every meaningful experience leaves us with learning and insight that allows us to bring more value to our clients. Whether it's overcoming enormous challenge, like the loss of a loved one, or it's a joyful experience like an amazing adventure in a land far away, we bring all that we learn and experience to our work. It gives us depth, insight, and wisdom, and the first way to start to harness that for our work is to tell the experience story

THE FORMULA

Part 1
The context

- We begin the experience story by describing the situation before the event. What was the "normal" before the unexpected thing happened. This description should feel very familiar to the audience; when we understand the context, we are primed to really see the shift that happens when things change. It's the moment before the world turned upside down. It feels constant and sure, which is part of why what comes next is so unsettling.

Part 2
The dramatic occurrence

- The next thing that happens in the experience story is the dramatic occurrence. Simply put, this is when something happens that is personal and challenging. Suddenly we see the world in a different way, and it can never return to what was. It's very important to describe this dramatic event clearly. When I say it's "personal," I mean that it feels like it's happening to us. It's not a random event that doesn't matter; it's something that will change the way we see, feel, or understand our world. It's a big shift and we need to first take it in and understand the implications of such a seismic change.

Part 3
The outcome of the event

- The final part of the experience story is when we share the outcome of what happened and how it impacted us. This is the opportunity to share how we harnessed our strengths so that we could not just cope but come through it strong. It's the way that we demonstrate our resilience, and it gives the audience the sense that maybe they could do it too. Maybe they have more strength and resilience than they thought. This is why the experience story can be inspiring and motivating.

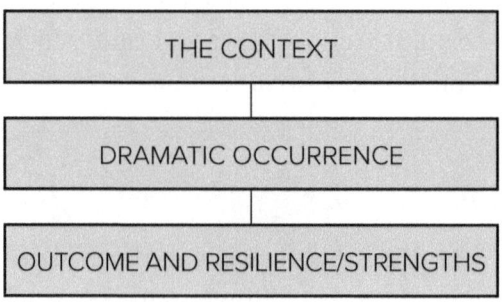

Examples

Lisa's Story

I had been raising my babies, and slowly tinkering with my business. I managed to get a client here and there and I was hired to speak a few times. I'd started to think about a website, but it was all very slow and there wasn't a lot of growth. I had lots of ideas and I was quite diligent about following through on creative projects, but I was not consistent about getting clients.

Then my partner was given two weeks' notice from the job that was supporting us. I had thought the writing was on the wall with his job for quite some time, but we had been ignoring it. He had no plan B. Neither of us did. During the next six months he tried to figure out what to do but there were not a lot of similar jobs out there, and he was fed up with his career path anyway.

I met with a friend one morning for coffee. As usual, I was talking about my partner, his dilemma about what he was going to do, and the increasing pressure to figure out how we were going to support our family. That's when I realized that, subconsciously, I had been waiting for him to figure things out while I was just letting things roll over in my business. It seemed that I had been acting like my coaching was more of a hobby than an actual business and it was time to make it work. For years I had been encouraging him to leave the job he didn't like, and telling him that it would be okay, that my business was growing. So here I was trying to support him to find his way while totally losing mine. My business wasn't growing, I was too distracted by his situation and the growing discomfort and uncertainty. It was time to make a change.

From that moment, my attitude and my commitment changed. I began to reach out to contacts and colleagues. I started to hustle. I found some opportunities and I created some more. And it worked. Over the next two years, I built a substantial business, and I've never looked back!

Jennifer's Story

I was on a stellar career path, meeting everyone's expectations, and climbing the corporate ladder. I liked the work and was happy to put in long hours. That winter I had traveled to attend a conference. The days were long and intense. I was tired. It was the end of the second day of the event, and I had just come back to my hotel room after dinner. I jumped into the shower; the water felt blissful. I could feel the tension drain away, but I was so tired. That's when I found the lump. It was unmistakable. Within a few days, my surgery was scheduled. It was confirmed as the worst kind, and the treatments began right away.

I couldn't believe that this was happening to me. I was fit and reasonably healthy, I ate well and had stopped smoking soon after I started, decades before. I made sure to get enough sleep and I exercised regularly. It just didn't make sense. Was this it? Is this how the story ends? It took weeks for it to sink in.

There were a lot of scary moments that year. There were days when I wasn't sure I was going to make it. There were moments when I wasn't even sure I wanted to. I lost many people who I had considered friends and others became friends for life, more like family. I learned how to live, not just how to avoid dying. I got through it, and in truth, it was a gift. I have a lot of changes because of my journey with cancer.

Jake's Story

We had been partying all week on the island and it was wild. We were young and free, with more money than sense. We had rented the coolest sports car and we felt like we were kings. That day we'd slept all morning, recovering from the revelry of the night before. We needed some milk and I said I'd go. I jumped into the car and sped down the road to the local store. The truck coming in the opposite direction didn't have a chance, and neither did I. The car flipped twice and stopped just a few feet short of the edge of the ravine. It could have ended very differently. With just a broken arm and a slight concussion, I was the luckiest guy in the world. The accident changed me. I kept wondering, If I had died, what difference would I have made in the world? I was just this stupid twenty-year-old kid who knew nothing and had done nothing. That's what started me on the path of self-development and professional development. Years later, I'm passionate about mentorship for young men. I'm an inspirational speaker and mentor for men under twenty-five. There is so much more that they can be in the world; they don't need to risk their life to discover that.

WHAT TO EXPECT

When you can share a powerful experience story you connect with your prospect at the heart level. They understand that you've been through something intense and challenging that changed you. It made a difference in your life. They also see that you have prevailed and that you have gained knowledge and wisdom because of this experience.

Sharing your experience is the opportunity to inspire others, not by bragging or feeling superior to others but by being willing to share your vulnerability. We don't want to be vulnerable for the sake of vulnerability but instead to share some of the most important moments in our lives because it is deeply connecting. When you share like this, you allow people to see your strength, your resilience, and your ability to see it through, to survive. That's what we all want. To see it in others and to believe it for ourselves.

Don't worry if you feel that your experience hasn't been dramatic enough. In truth (and thankfully) we haven't all had these near-death experiences that others talk about. Remember, I started out worrying that I wouldn't be able to tell good stories because my life is not that interesting. It still isn't! But our experiences are often profound and moving and very accessible to others, so trust that you have these stories inside you. I promise you, you do!

Here's the template of the Experience Story so you can get started!

The Formula

We start by describing the situation before the event, the context. Then there is a dramatic unexpected occurrence that is personal and challenging. We need to describe it clearly. The outcome of the story shows us our resilience and helps us step into our strengths.

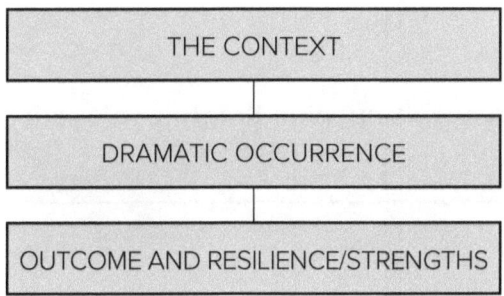

It was a time when I was _____

_____

[share context, life situation, work-related challenges or assumptions].

It happened at this specific time/place/event _____

_____

The event that changed everything _____

_____

[dramatic event like change in relationship status, work disaster, personal challenges, etc.].

Describe specific event with details _____

_____

Chapter 10: The Experience Story

My immediate reaction was _____

_____

Over time, I realized that _____

_____

[insights about the situation].

I now knew that I could _____

_____

[insights about yourself].

From that time on, I was able to _____

_____

[application of all the insights to your life and work].

CHAPTER 11
The Failure Story

"It is impossible to live without failing at something unless you live so cautiously that you might as well not have lived at all, in which case you have failed by default."

—J.K. ROWLING, author

THIS IS THE STORY that surfaces the pain and the shame of when things did not work out as planned. It's a story that is full of vulnerability. It's not an easy story to tell but it's a very important one because it's where your humanity shows up. In truth, we all make mistakes and we all fail, so being able to tell this story makes you more accessible and even more likeable. On hearing your failure story, the prospective client thinks, "If you're willing to share this story, then perhaps I don't need to feel such shame about the failures I've experienced."

WHAT IS THIS STORY?

The Failure Story is the story of when you experienced something that went very wrong. It shows the inevitability of making mistakes, no matter how prepared you think you are, how good you are at what you do, and how committed you are to your desired outcome. There can be no predicting certain failures; as one of my entrepreneur colleagues said to me after I had experienced a colossal failure, "It happens to the best of us!"

The Failure Story should always include how you picked yourself up, brushed yourself off, and started all over.

WHY SHOULD WE TELL IT?

This is the ultimate story of sharing that you are a real person, you make mistakes, things go wrong, life happens, but you can still work things out and keep going. As such, it reveals your humanity and makes you so much more relatable. If you're willing to admit failure and even share the story, then I trust that when I make a mistake it will be understood and accepted as part of the process.

The Failure Story also demonstrates your perseverance and commitment to getting the job done. It tells your prospects that you'll stick around, that you'll be there through thick and thin, that what to expect is not all roses but you've got their back.

You often hear people say that failure is important because it's a great teacher. That it's through failure that we learn what not to do and how not to act. They say that failure is the precursor to success. However, many of these people don't share their own examples of failure, nor do they explain how hard it is. One of my corporate clients used to talk like this all the time, yet I noticed they only seemed to tell the "hero" stories, the times when things went exceptionally well. When I asked why, they admitted that this level of vulnerability was not really part of their culture. That's when we began to see why there was a lack of trust between management and employees.

The Failure Story is a powerful connector between you and your prospect (or in the case above, between you and your team). It shows your humility, your fallibility, and your resilience. If you can get through this difficult situation, you can guide others through something difficult and they don't have to be afraid anymore. They can fail, admit it, work through it, and be supported. That means people become more fearless in the work they do and the risks they take. This often results in much better outcomes. This is such an important story.

THE FORMULA

Part 1
Confidence

- The Failure Story usually starts with a presumption of success. The outcome you are going for is a given. You are quite sure of what is about to happen next, and you are assured that everything is on track. You have a strong belief that all will be well. It always begins with unwavering confidence in the reality you see around you so that you have no reason to be concerned. The fact that the idea you have might fail doesn't even occur to you.

Part 2
The failure

- The next part of this story is when the unexpected happens: the thing you were so sure of actually fails. At first you are surprised and shocked. You're not even sure what happened, and you don't quite believe it. Once you see that this is the reality, that things have gone really wrong, that's when the pain and shame sneak in. You begin to realize the impact of your failure and you can't believe that you allowed it to happen; you're shocked that this is your new reality. It hurts and you can't imagine how you'll ever tell anyone or what people will think about you when they find out.

Part 3

The recovery

- Finally, the Failure Story delves into what you did to get back up again. It describes what you had to do to keep going, how it felt and the price you had to pay. The recovery from your failure is often a moment of humility as the lesson of the failure starts to sink in. This lesson is gold—it's the way you turn the whole experience around. In truth, maybe people who have experienced failure have later come to believe that it was the making of them. At the same time, it's important not to underplay how painful failure can be, how debilitating and shameful it feels. But this is not usually lasting; often we can transcend the pain and the shame because the learning is so much more empowering. That's the true goal of sharing the Failure Story—to be able to transcend the emotional trap that failure can be, while at the same time inspiring others to do the same. And to learn the practical, valuable lessons along the way!

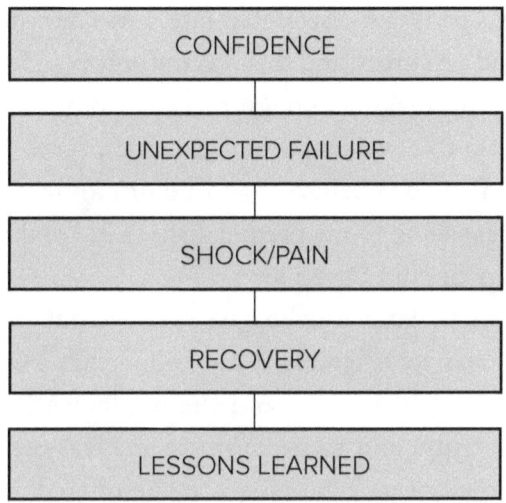

Examples

Lisa's Story

I had been in business for several years and had a steady flow of clients, though my revenue was somewhat unpredictable. It was time to launch a new program. I was excited about it; I felt like it was time to play bigger. I designed the program, hired a copywriter to help with the marketing, and had a few people who were willing to send out an email to their audience for me too. I was ready to welcome tons of people into this new program. The big day arrived and the emails started to go out.

I had planned a webinar to introduce people to the idea and I had quite a few people show up for that. But pretty soon, it became clear that something wasn't working. Or perhaps lots of things weren't working. Instead of thirty people registering for my program as I had planned, three signed up. And of those three, one was a friend who was getting a discounted rate. I was devastated. I had invested time and resources, and this was my only plan for the business. I was banking on making enough revenue from this program that I would be able to cover important expenses, some of which were already spent. I couldn't believe it and I didn't know how I would go on. I remember saying to my partner, "That's it, I'm done. Maybe it's time to give up. Should I get a job?"

A few weeks later a colleague reached out to ask how the launch was. I was so ashamed of my failure that I was tempted to lie, to tell her that it was fine and the results were good. Instead, I told her the truth, and to my surprise she was really supportive. "It happens to all of us," she said, and she offered to help me understand what had gone wrong and design a better marketing plan for next time. In truth, I learned a lot from that failed launch and that has helped me do much better since then. But it also taught me that I'm not alone in getting things wrong and with the help of good people, I'm able to keep going, to find the right way and to make the business work.

Tanya's Story

I was in the public sector for years, going between various government jobs and educational institutions. I had a great reputation, and I really knew how to build educational programs. When I left my job to go out on my own, I knew the exact program I needed to build. I spent the next eighteen months researching, designing, and building the perfect program. It had the topic covered perfectly. When I started to think about selling it, I wasn't quite sure who would be interested. For the next eight months I knocked on doors, reached out to all my contacts, and though everyone was very friendly and encouraging, that was it. They said they liked the idea, but no one wanted to buy my perfect program.

Eventually I realized that I had created it in a bubble; I had no client data that pointed to this particular type of intervention. I had designed the entire thing in my head and it looked like there was no real demand for it. I was so disappointed. I would need to start all over. But next time I did it very differently. I spoke to my audience, figured out what they wanted, and ended up selling the idea before I had even created the program—what a difference! My business is finally taking off.

Ben's Story

I left my corporate job because I was fed up with the hours and the stress and I really wanted to be my own boss. I also loved the idea of becoming a coach. So I took a few courses and started telling people about my new direction. Weeks and months went by and I took one course after another to try to learn about how to find clients. One would tell me to create a Facebook group, another to learn how to make great videos but I was all over the place and the clients weren't showing up. After two years, I had exhausted all my savings and had borrowed a significant amount from my brother. The worst thing was, I was so deeply ashamed that I just couldn't get this business going.

That's when I realized that it was make-or-break. I had been following a really interesting company online and they were offering a mentorship program. Everything they said made sense, but more importantly I felt that I could trust them. I signed up. This would be my very last attempt to make this thing work. And it did. I was so thrilled and so relieved. After going through their program several times, I filled my practice and had a waiting list. I knew this program worked—it had changed my life—and I was excited to help others do the same. I started telling people all about it but then I knew I wanted more. So I became certified in their methodology and now I help other coaches who want to build their business. It's so thrilling to help them thrive in the way that I did when I had the right advice and support.

WHAT TO EXPECT

When you share your failure story, you become instantly more relatable. The potential client can see that you were once in their shoes and you are not afraid to both share your mistakes and learn from them. This means you become more appealing to your prospects as a potential guide that can help them navigate through similar situations and either recover from failure or avoid it altogether.

Sharing your failure story tells your prospects that you've put in the hard work, you've dealt with tough situations, and you've managed to recover from them. From this kind of sharing, they understand that they can trust you to see them through tough times too. You won't give up, and you won't shame them or laugh at them for getting things wrong. You'll be there to help them come through, stand their ground, and make the business work.

Here's the template of the Failure Story so you can get started!

Chapter 11: The Failure Story

The Formula

The Failure Story begins with a presumption of success. You start by sharing how you seemed so confident, that you were sure of your ability to do well and had no inclination that failure was even possible. Then the unexpected failure happens, and you share the surprise and the pain. Finally, the Failure Story describes what you did to get back up again, to keep going, and the lesson you learned.

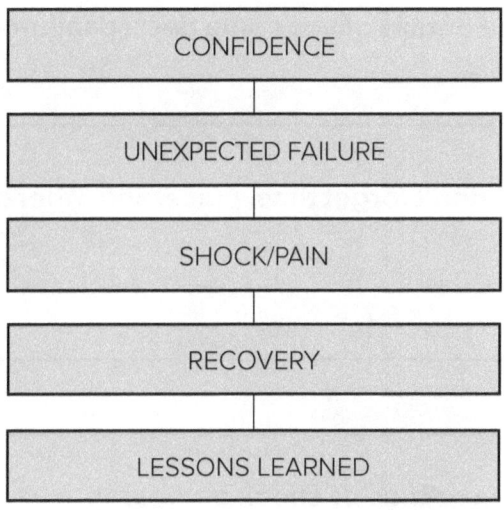

I always knew that I could _____

_____

[confidence around a specific situation, ability, or assumptions of how things work].

Describe the details of your unexpected failure _____

_____

[be specific, don't forget time, place, and other descriptors].

I felt _____

_____

[explore the feelings of shock and pain].

Chapter 11: The Failure Story

Over the next few days/weeks/years _____

_____

[what recovery looked like; don't overdramatize or exaggerate but also don't gloss over the challenges you faced].

What I discovered was _____

_____

[your insights and new understandings as a result of the failure].

And that means that _____

_____

[how you and your business have changed as a result of your insights].

I am now committed to _____

_____

[how your focus or commitments may have changed].

CHAPTER 12

The Vision Story

> *"To succeed . . . you need to find something to hold on to, something to motivate you, something to inspire you."*
>
> —Tony Dorsett, NFL player

WHEN YOU ARTICULATE your vision story, it allows the client to envision their own future, to connect with a better world for themselves too.

WHAT IS THIS STORY?

The Vision Story is the story that helps you create a clear picture of what you desire, in your business, for yourself, and for the world. It is aspirational and it also inspires both you and your client to see how the world can be transformed by the work you are committed to. Often the Vision Story is deeply personal, and it can also be very practical. For example, when I started my business, part of my vision was to be available for my kids, to create a lifestyle that allowed me the flexibility and freedom to have a very specific kind of family life. For others the Vision Story may be about legacy, the kind of world they want to leave behind when their time is done (none of us are getting any younger!). Sometimes the Vision Story is about the money they want to make, or the places they want to see. Often it's about the impact people want to make in a very specific area of their life, or a topic they are passionate about.

The Vision Story holds space for the possibility of what you can build and create; it's the dreaming space but it should also be deeply related to reality. This isn't about dreaming of the impossible; it's about envisioning a better world while being committed to this improved future.

The Vision Story is a story of hope, and we all need that! While wars rage and crises continue, we need to be able to see something better, to imagine a way of being that is peaceful and whole. The Vision Story is a powerful motivator—it's a story that keeps us moving forward and striving for improvement. When we can see the possibility of this better future, this story is the promise that if we keep the story clear and work hard, we will indeed be able to create something wonderful, and impact others to do the same. It's as much a reminder and a motivator for us, the storytellers, as it is for our clients and followers.

THE FORMULA

Part 1
What if

- Once you have introduced the context, the Vision Story has a simple formula that begins with "what if" or "imagine." This makes the Vision Story somewhat more whimsical by nature, but don't be mistaken that this is some sort of magical thinking and just flippant imagining. The Vision Story must be grounded in reality and possible to attain, even if it feels almost like daring to believe in the impossible. We do get bogged down in reality and stodgy thinking at times, so this story is the opportunity to think big and really imagine what's possible—it's exciting.

Part 2
Tangible details

- Once we have our "what if" statement, we need to add tangible details to make the story feel real. It's not enough to imagine the impossible—we need to add real steps to take to show that it can be attained. We must ground the Vision Story in the day-to-day details that allow us to really see it so that we can believe it to be possible.

Part 3
Invitation

- Part of making the Vision Story work is to enroll ourselves and others into the possibility. If it's not grounded then it simply won't work, and people won't believe you. So the final part of the formula is the invitation to step into the story. We invite others to help us co-create this vision by participating in the future story. This is how the Vision Story really comes alive!

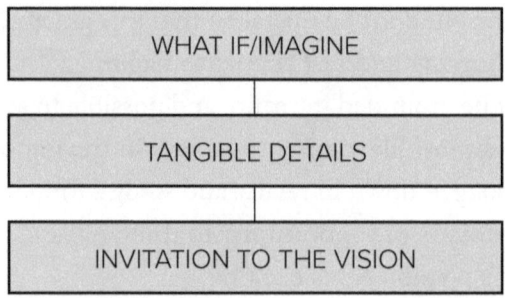

Examples

Lisa's Story

What if you could reach out to potential clients and they immediately wanted to work with you? What if your ideal clients found you—yes, that's right, they heard about you and came looking for you.

I had just finished my coaching course. I was newly certified as a professional coach and yet I couldn't find any clients. It seems that they don't teach that part in coach school. And it was really hard. I'm guessing that was the same for you too. I kept wondering, How do I find great clients? What do I need to do to have a full, thriving practice?

Around the time that I had been in coach training, I had also studied to become a professional storyteller. I noticed that the skills I gained in storytelling could be helpful for building my business. I saw that when I told a great story, people remembered the story and they remembered the way it made them feel. They remembered me too. So it made sense that if I could tell a compelling story about my business, then people would connect with me more, and that would be good for business.

It works. When you start telling compelling stories about what you do, people notice—they self-select and come looking for you. It's an easy, powerful way to attract clients, and you too can learn it!

Chapter 12: The Vision Story

Julie's Story

For years, I struggled when buying produce that I could tell had been grown with toxins and in a manner that was damaging to the environment. It really bothered me, but I wasn't a farmer, and I didn't know what difference I could make. Then I asked myself, What if I could source organic produce and make it affordable for my local community? I'm not an activist and yet I couldn't let go of this vision. Well, I did some research and found that there were many farmers in our region who were interested in getting access to customers like me. I organized a local farmer's market and it's really taken off. First, I've completely changed how I shop and how I eat. I feel healthier and so much more aligned with my values. And I'm helping others do the same. What if you could revolutionize your local community while improving your health and that of your family? Let's connect and see how you can join the movement.

Jonathan's Story

I stopped eating meat when I was twelve and had watched my mother prepare a meal of beef. I just couldn't help thinking about the cows. When we got a dog that year, I could see how emotionally attached she was to me, so how could an animal even bigger not have feelings? I just couldn't bear it and never ate meat again. As an adult, I see that many people feel the same way but just can't imagine their life without meat. Well, I can help you navigate that. You can make healthy, varied meals that are so delicious, you'll never again have to compromise your beliefs about animal cruelty or the impact of the meat industry on our environment. With a step-by-step plan to living without having to consume animal products, you'll feel freedom and health you've never imagined possible.

WHAT TO EXPECT

When you have a powerful vision story, you become a huge inspiration to others. So many people spend their lives complaining about all the wrongs in their world—all the things that they wish were different but somehow don't feel empowered to change them. When you can envision a different future and make it a real possibility, when you can show people the steps they need to take to change their reality, this is massively powerful. When people can see a better future and understand the steps that they need to take to achieve the outcomes they desire, they instinctively trust that you are the person to take them there.

Not only do you make a huge impression on people with your vision, your brilliance, and what you have achieved, but you also make it real for them. And you inspire others to take action. From the perspective of your business, this means that they are inspired to hire you or buy your service.

Here's the template of the Vision Story so you can get started!

The Formula

The Vision Story has a simple formula that starts with "what if" or "imagine." It's perhaps more whimsical by nature and yet must be grounded and clear in order to have impact. Once we have our "what if" statement, we need to add tangible details to make the story feel real. The final part of the formula is the invitation to co-create this vision through participation.

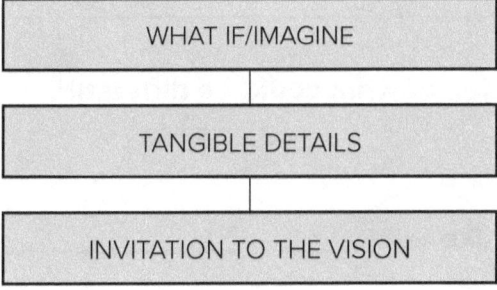

It all started when _____

_____

[set the context through time, place, and current situation].

But I realized that _____

_____

[the realization of what could be different].

It would be like this _____

_____

[describe the details of your vision].

Can you imagine what your life/business would be like if

_____

[describe how it would look for them]?

Chapter 12: The Vision Story

My invitation to you is _____

_____

[give details of what you expect, invite, and anticipate for them if they take up the challenge].

CHAPTER 13
The Proof Story

"People who say it cannot be done should not interrupt those who are doing it."
—GEORGE BERNARD SHAW, playwright

THIS STORY ADDS color, texture, and of course credibility to the kind of work you do and the outcomes you can get for your clients. One thing that's very important about the Proof Story is not to get caught up in the process of the work you do, but instead to make sure that the outcomes are the focus.

WHAT IS THIS STORY?

The Proof Story is a story that you tell to describe the client's experience working with you. Or it could be a story told by clients in the form of a testimonial. The Proof Story is one of the most persuasive stories in your business because it literally proves that your service or program works. The story paints a vivid picture of how you have already supported people to get the results that you promise. Whether it's told by you (about the client) or by the client (as a testimonial), the Proof Story is the voice of the people who have been impacted by your work.

The Proof Story should include not just the experience of the client but also the tangible results they got from the work with you.

WHY SHOULD WE TELL IT?

Most people who are considering investing in a service or program have a few simple questions. They wonder, Does this service or program work? They also ask, Will it work for me? Your proof story will give tangible evidence that what you do works for the specific person that the story describes. Ideally this person will be similar to or resonate with the client you want to attract. When your ideal client hears this story, they identify with the client you describe and are delighted with the result they have achieved. We want that prospect to think, "If it worked for them, it will work for me too."

The Proof Story should be clear, detailed, and outcome focused. When the story describes your target client and speaks to their greatest needs and desires, it feels like the proof they need to believe that they can also experience this kind of transformation. When the Proof Story describes, in detail, the outcomes and result of your work in a tangible, clear way, it's the stamp of approval the person needs to take a chance and move forward to hire you.

THE FORMULA

Part 1

Context/situation

- The Proof Story should start by describing the situation before the work began, helping your prospect recognize themselves and their concerns in your client's story. They should feel like you're describing their situation. You need to dig deep into their challenge or their pain so that they can feel the gap between where they are right now and what they most desire to change.

Part 2

What you did

- This is the part of the Proof Story where you share how you worked together so that the prospective client understands the impact you've had as you provided the service. What you did with your client is an important part of the Proof Story. You need to highlight the difference between what the client did before and what changed while they were working with you. This is so that the prospect can come to the correct conclusion that the great outcome was as a result of the work you did together. (You'd be surprised how many people don't make this connection!)

Part 3

Tangible results

- The final part of the Proof Story must be tangible, showing the real-life impact the work had for your client. It's not just about feeling better (though that's a great outcome too), but you need to demonstrate all the ways that the client has been transformed by the work. Ideally, you want to lean into the three most important needs and desires that people have. These are the needs in relation to money, time, and health. If you can prove that your work resulted in an increase in revenue (or saving of expenses), you must share that. If you see that your client saved time or saw meaningful improvement in their health, then these stories will be hugely influential.

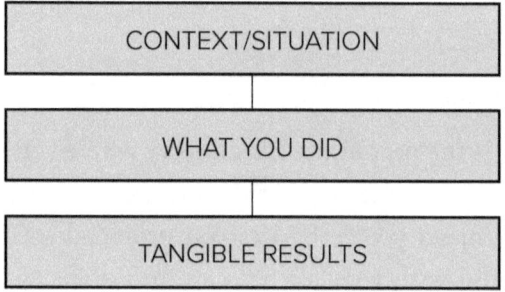

Examples

Lisa's Story

Susan was starting her coaching and consulting business and was full of doubt about her credibility and relatability for her target audience. She had worked for years in a corporation, starting her career as an assistant and working right up to senior leadership. By all accounts, she had a stunning career. However, when it came to talking about her services as a coach and consultant, she was racked with doubts.

We worked together and I helped her see that the professional experience in her career was directly related to her current coaching offering. We looked at all the times she had trained, coached, and mentored during her time in the corporation. She recalled how often she was sought out for support and advice, so much more than any of her colleagues. With that clarity, we worked on the stories she could tell in her meetings, her materials, and her networking to speak to all of this amazing experience. Her outlook and confidence completely changed. She started to feel excited about sharing her work with prospects. Within three months, her business was at capacity, and she had to start a waiting list for clients!

Craig's Story

When Janet came to work with me, she had clients but was exhausted and almost burned out. At that time, she only worked with clients one-on-one. She had thought about creating a group coaching offer but felt that she didn't have the time, energy, or clarity to move forward with it. She was beginning to question if this whole business was the right path for her. She would finish her days exhausted, depleted, and without any time for herself or her family. It was unsustainable.

When we started working together, I wanted to address the ideas that she had about group coaching and other ways to leverage her time and energy. She desperately needed to change the way she worked. Very quickly we restructured her one-on-one offerings, increased her prices, created a waiting list, and explored different ways she could offer value to her clients. Within six months, she was working five hours less per week and had increased her revenue by 20 percent—and we were only getting started!

Angela's Story

When Mona came to see me, she had tried every diet you can imagine. She had gone up and down in weight for years, and for every pound she lost, she seemed to gain several more. She had pretty much given up, but then she had a medical checkup and realized that she was on the path to becoming dependent upon heart and diabetes medication. This was getting beyond just feeling uncomfortable with her size—now she was getting sick. We started working on her day-to-day habits and activities. More importantly, we started uncovering the eating culture and emotional landscape she had grown up in. Slowly we began to debunk the beliefs she had about herself, her weight, and her well-being. It wasn't a quick fix, but after six months she had shed twenty pounds and was just getting started. She was thrilled because she knew that she had a whole new outlook on life, more energy, and more freedom, and she didn't have to worry about medication anymore. She was healthier than she had been in years.

WHAT TO EXPECT

The Proof Story is a great driver for decision-making. Often a prospect will deliberate about working with you for quite some time. They run through the pros and cons and never quite land on whether they believe that the program or service will work for them. When they hear a proof story, it's often the moment that they decide to go ahead. Now they can see the true stories of those who have been impacted by the work and it's the tipping point to get them to take the next step.

The Proof Story is so important that you'll need to have several proof stories on your website and your sales page, and also have them ready to tell. This means that you always want to be collecting testimonials and client experiences. They are such a powerful and persuasive resource in your business.

Here's the template of the Proof Story so you can get started!

The Formula

The Proof Story should start by describing the situation before the work began, helping your prospect recognize themselves and their 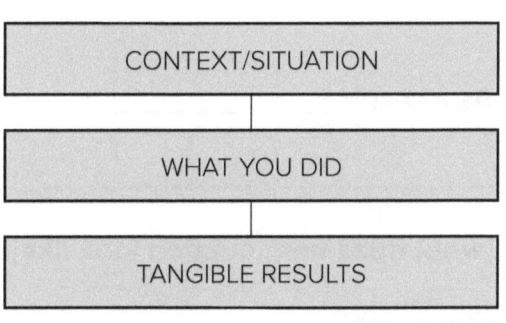 concerns in your client's story. They should feel like you're describing their situation. Then you give the details of how you worked together and what happened as a result. This final part should be tangible, showing the real-life impact the work had for your client. Ideally, if you can speak to increases in revenue, savings, time, or health, this is highly desirable.

My client [x] was _____

_____

[describe her situation before you began to work together]

During our work she_____

_____

[detail what you did together....]

As a result _____

_____

[what does her situation look like now, what were the outcomes]

CHAPTER 14

Wrapping Up

> *"The more you practice, the better you become.*
> *The better you become, the more freedom you have to create."*
>
> —RICKY GERVAIS, comedian, actor, quoted in
> *Scientific American: Mind*

THE VP OF HUMAN RESOURCES I had once worked with called me to ask about coaching their CEO. She said he desperately needed to get some support to help him with some speaking engagements coming up but also, in general, he wanted to learn about leadership presence. I was excited—that's the work I love to do most! She invited me to meet with him and discuss the possibility of doing a coaching engagement.

We met in his office, and before he arrived I had the chance to look at the amazing photography that was all over the walls. I was standing looking at a gorgeous shot, a silhouette of a child by the ocean. "That was in Mali," he said, "when I traveled through Africa."

"It's beautiful," I replied—a good way to start the interview. I asked him to tell me about himself, the company, and what he was looking for.

He spoke for quite some time, telling me about his career experience, the amazing travel he had done, and his passion for cooking and photography. Then he shared how he felt when he spoke on stages and the feedback he'd been given by colleagues and advisors; there was certainly work to be done. When he finished speaking, he said to me, "So what do you do, and what does it cost?"

I took a deep breath and said, "Can I tell you a little about me?"

"Of course!" he said.

And so I spent a few minutes telling my story and focusing on the experiences that most closely matched the things that he had told me about himself and his interests. I shared that I had worked on cruise ships as a photographer, that I love working with multi-talented and passionate leaders and gave some examples of the people and organizations I'd worked with. I shared a story about a leader I had worked with who had struggled with some of the things he described about himself. And I made sure to include the outcome of the work we had done together—that he felt more confident, more relaxed, and more impactful on the stage and in his leadership as a result of the work we did together.

When I finished speaking, the CEO said to me, "Awesome, I'm in. When do we start?" I didn't have to talk about the cost of my service or anything else, he was sold!

When you can tell the stories that your business needs, you have an incredible way to sell without selling your soul or even feeling like you're selling, to persuade without manipulation, to impact without stress.

The key to selling your services is selling through story. Now you have the tools to do just that. Take each of the seven stories in this book and work on them, master them, and begin to tell them.

Chapter 14: Wrapping Up

They won't be perfect at first, but that's fine. There is an important ingredient you need to add, but to reveal this I need to tell you another story!

I was asked to facilitate an important meeting of the senior team. My boss was the senior VP and he needed to participate in the discussions, so I was next in line to make this meeting go smoothly. The morning arrived; we were in a hotel because they believed that would help them be more focused, less distracted, and more able to get the work done.

My boss said to me, "Let's start with a SWOT analysis." I looked at him blankly, thinking, What is that? He took me aside and drew a big cross on a piece of paper and explained, "Four boxes: strengths, weaknesses, opportunities, and threats—you got it." I recovered fast. Yes, I had it. In truth, I'd learned about the SWOT analysis during my MBA classes. I had even done an exam about it, but in the moment I had totally forgotten. Well, I can tell you, I never again forgot what a SWOT analysis was. Here's the thing—you can read a book or take a class, you can learn a formula, but none of it works unless you use the tool.

So that's the missing ingredient: telling the stories. You need to practice and practice, to go out and tell your stories, and then tell them again. Believe me, your stories will change over time as you have more experiences and think of more pivotal moments that you can tell. And that's perfect. The most important thing is to keep going, keep crafting, keep telling your amazing stories!

Additional resources to support you

DOWNLOAD THE AUDIOBOOK AND THE SEVEN STORIES TOOLKIT (FOR FREE)!

Just to say thank you for reading my book, I'd love to share the audiobook version PLUS the accompanying Seven Stories Toolkit, at no cost whatsoever—it's my gift to you.

www.story-coach.com/7-stories-toolkit

Acknowledgments

WHEN PEOPLE ASK ME if I love writing, I have to admit that I most love having written. The act of writing can be excruciating, but I'm so happy that when I'm in the zone, the writing does flow. The zone only shows up when I have a backdrop of the work I get to do with the amazing clients I've been so honored to serve. So thank you to all my clients, individuals and organizations, teams, leaders, and entrepreneurs who have been the playground for learning and teaching. Thanks to all of you who have shared your stories, even the ones that are as hard to live as they are to tell.

Huge thanks to Danny Iny, my mentor, for always setting high bars for me to reach and being willing to drag me some of the way when necessary. And thanks to all the Mirasee team, who live their values and provide a backdrop of optimism and talent, commitment, and support—you're awesome, and it's a thrill to work with you.

Thanks to Ally Machate and the team at The Writer's Ally for all your help to get this book published.

Huge appreciation to Ilan, my love, and our boys for putting up with long hours while I work and write. I can't tell you how much it means to me when there is someone to drop in a cup of tea, fix a salad, or go for a long walk and listen to, yes, more stories. Boys, I am so in awe of the young men you have become. Your courage, strength, and kindness bowls me over again and again. I'm so blessed to have you in my life. You are my greatest inspiration.

Bibliography

Baldwin, Christina. *StoryCatcher: Making Sense of Our Lives Through the Power and Practice of Story.* New World Library, 2007.

Chip and Dan Heath, *Made to Stick: Why Some Ideas Survive and Others Die,* Random House, 2007

Cox, Allison M., and David H. Albert. *The Healing Hearts Families: Storytelling to Encourage Caring and Healthy Families.* New Society Publishers, 2003.

Dicks, Matthew. *StoryWorthy: Engage, Teach, Persuade, and Change Your Life through the Power of Storytelling.* New World Library, 2018.

Duarte, Nancy. Resonate: Present Visual Stories that Transform Audiences. Wiley, 2010.

Helm Meade, Erica. *The Moon in the Well: Wisdom Tales to Transform Your Life, Family and Community.* Open Court Publishing, 2001.

Mellon, Nancy, and Ashley Ramsden. *Body Eloquence: The Power of Myth and Story to Awaken the Body's Energies.* Energy Psychology Press, 2008.

Simmons, Annette. *The Story Factor: Inspiration, Influence and Persuasion Through the Art of Storytelling.* Basic Books, 2000, revised 2019.

Simms, Laura. *Our Secret Territory: The Essence of Storytelling.* First Sentient Publications, 2011.

About the Author

LISA BLOOM, founder of Story Coach, works with organizations developing leaders, creative yet resilient cultures, and leading powerful change processes with the power of storytelling. She works with entrepreneurs and business owners to help them find confidence, attract ideal clients, and find their success story. And she trains coaches to use storytelling as a powerful approach to impact their clients and grow their business.

Lisa is a professional storyteller, accredited coach, author, mentor, and leadership expert. Her groundbreaking techniques have enabled her to grow her business and take to the stage, where she speaks internationally about this approach to business, leadership, and coaching.

Lisa is also the director of the ACES Business Acceleration Program for Mirasee, working with a team of coaches to support entrepreneurs to build successful online businesses.

ON A MORE PERSONAL NOTE

Lisa grew up in Dublin, Ireland, surrounded by the beautiful countryside (it really is greener than anywhere else!), amazing stories of pixies and leprechauns, and the warmth of Jewish tradition and practice. She traveled for several years working as waitress, stable girl, galley slave, bartender, and photographer with degree and secretarial skills in hand.

Later she worked for the United States Agency for International Development (USAID) at the most exciting of times, on development programs in the West Bank and Gaza. During this time, she volunteered in a rape crisis center, completed a Boston University MBA, and married Ilan.

They moved to Ireland for a few years, where they grew professionally. Lisa worked in large multinational organizations, realizing her passion in learning and development management. These years were filled with personal development, coaching training, ICF accreditation, and the birth of Story Coach Ltd.

Lisa, Ilan, and their four sons have made their home in the beautiful hills of Zichron Ya'acov in the north of Israel, where she continues to serve international clients, write books, and tell stories!

www.ingramcontent.com/pod-product-compliance
Lightning Source LLC
LaVergne TN
LVHW041950070526
838199LV00051BA/2974